THE

COMPREHENSIVE

ENGLISH GRAMMAR,

THEORETICAL & PRACTICAL.

BY

DAVID CLARK,

*Of the London University, Principal of Albion House School,
Brierly Hill, Staffordshire.*

THE EDUCATIONAL TRADING COMPANY,

LIMITED,

LONDON, BIRMINGHAM, AND BRISTOL.

—

1871.

CONTENTS.

CONTENTS.

PREFACE.

A somewhat lengthened experience in practical tuition has led me to believe that it is possible to present the facts and principles of English Grammar in a more logical and orderly manner than yet given in any book with which I am acquainted.

A rage has recently sprung up for explaining minutely in books the principles of English Grammar; hence, a host of Explanatory English Grammars has lately appeared. With all deference to the abilities of the writers of such books, I humbly submit that those who expect to make grammar explain itself to youthful minds by means of books, attempt the impossible. Grammar can only be explained to youth by the living voice of the teacher, and the man who relies on any other method had better change his occupation at once. Besides, such books are usually such a huddled-up store of grammatical confusion, that to attempt to find any fact or principle in them in answer to a given question, would be almost a hopeless task.

What is wanted in a school grammar is a complete, orderly, and logical arrangement of its various parts, equally adapted to class study and reference.

The treatment of the different parts of speech follows the natural order of *definition, classification, inflection,* where these severally exist; and notwithstanding the deviation from the practice of some recent and distinguished writers on the subject, I have, after the most careful consideration, given these under a single heading, rather than treated inflection by itself. Little is gained, and much lost, in my opinion, by such an arrangement.

The arrangement of the verb has been adopted after much thought, and a careful comparison of the most approved modern treatises. There are properly three *times* or tenses—present, past, and future, all others being subsidiary, and in a manner explanatory of them. These may therefore properly be considered as *primary*, the others as *secondary*, and should therefore be classed together. I leave out of sight altogether the weighty argument that Latin grammarians have adopted this course for an entirely different reason—the formation of the word.*

As to the definition of a verb here given, I may add that twenty years' experience has demonstrated that by no other can the character of the verb be so clearly explained to youthful minds. We have not improved upon the older grammarians in every particular.

Although, as Archbishop Trench says,† "It would be

* It is perhaps too much to expect that mankind will ever think or write alike on any particular whatever connected with this subject. The "glorious liberty" that exists in this country, where there is no *Academy* or other court possessing an appellate jurisdiction on the matter, has introduced the most "glorious" confusion, and even contradiction, into school grammars. This is a great evil, for it not only perplexes the pupil's mind by causing him to learn and unlearn afresh on every change of school, but leads him to question whether there is such a thing at all as grammatical truth. There is a gleam of hope, however, at least in one direction. The Public School Latin Primer, Smith's Principia Latina, and Bryce's First Latin Reader—works whose circulation is greater perhaps than all similar ones together—exhibit the Latin verb in the same order, and, as I have said, from the *formation of the word*. This may be said to decide the question as far as Latin is concerned; and as we have here two strong reasons for such an arrangement—*common sense* and *verbal formation*—it is to be hoped we are not far from unanimity on at least one point of grammatical arrangement.

† "English, Past and Present," p. 11.

curious to know how many have had their attention drawn to the fact that the subjunctive mood is at this very moment perishing in English," I have deemed it premature yet to omit it altogether.

The "Analysis of Sentences" will be found, it is believed, amply sufficient for the great majority of English students.

Without going into minor details, I may finally express my conviction that there are few questions put at the Matriculation or Middle-Class Examinations which will not be found answered in this book.

D. C.

ALBION HOUSE SCHOOL,
    BRIERLY HILL, 1871.

ERRATA.

From the change of page the Perfect Tense in page 19 should have been in the place of the Past Tense, page 20, and *vice versa.*

INTRODUCTION.

Mankind communicate their thoughts by means of *language*.

Language is either spoken or written.

Grammar is that science which treats of the principles and rules of language.

It is divided into four parts—*Orthography, Etymology, Syntax,* and *Prosody.*

CHAPTER I.

ORTHOGRAPHY.

LETTERS.

Orthography treats of *letters*, their sounds, and combinations into syllables and words.

Letters are divided into *vowels* and *consonants.*

A vowel has a full and complete sound of itself.

The vowels are *a, e, i, o, u;* and *w* and *y* when they do not begin a syllable.

The **consonant** cannot be distinctly sounded without the help of a vowel.

The consonants have been classed into :—

Aspirate, or breathing, as	*h.*
Guttural, or throat "	*k, g.*
Labial, or lip "	*p, b, f, v, m.*
Lingual, or tongue "	*t, d, s, z, l, r, n.*
Redundant "	*c, q, j, x.*

L, m, n, r are sometimes called *liquid,* from their readiness to combine with others.

A *diphthong* is the union of two vowels in one sound, as *aa, ae, ai, au, ea, ei, ee, ey, oe, oi, ou.*

A *triphthong* is the union of three vowels in one sound, as *eau* in beauty, beau; *iew* in view; *uoy* in buoy; *uay* in quay.

B

Exercise 1.

Point out diphthongs and triphthongs where they exist :—

Much, Baal, truth, land, care, beauty, laid, aged, buoy, large, again, merry, leaf, flambeaux, heir, hard, quay, hurt, interview, voice, away, from, sound, teach, fetch, Torquay, they, now, income, difficulties, honour, saviour.

SYLLABLES AND WORDS.

A **syllable** is a single utterance of the voice, and may consist of one or more letters. In every syllable there must be at least one vowel.

A word of one syllable is called a monosyllable, as *just ;* a word of two syllables, a dissyllable, as *justice ;* a word of three syllables, a trisyllable, as *justify ;* a word of four or more syllables, a polysyllable, as *justifying, justification.*

The general rule for dividing words into syllables is to begin each syllable with a consonant where possible, and where two consonants come together to separate them.

A word is formed of one or more syllables, and is either *primitive* or *derivative.*

A **primitive** word is derived from no other word, as *love, give.*

A **derivative** word is one derived from some other word, as *loving, giver.*

Derivatives are called **compound** when they are composed of two or more primitive or derivative words, as *mankind, foolhardy, cabinet-maker.*

Exercise 2.

Distinguish the following, (1) as to syllables, (2) as to primitive, derivative, and compound :—

Man, iniquity, rudeness, truth, constancy, manly, teach, breakfast, consternation, mankind, alliteration, but, truly, teapot, house, injury, help, household, son, beauty, landlord, indicate, helpful, general, great, battle-field, deadly, death-bed, employment, smoke-room.

CHAPTER III.

ETYMOLOGY.

Etymology treats of *words,* their classification, inflection, and derivation.

There are nine classes of words, or parts of speech—*Article, Noun, Adjective, Pronoun, Verb, Adverb, Preposition, Conjunction,* and *Interjection.*

An **article** is a word placed before a noun to limit its signification, as *a* man, *an* apple, *the* garden.

A **noun** is the name of any living being, place, thing, or quality, as *John, angel, London, desk, truth.*

An **adjective** is a word used to qualify a noun, as "*a good* boy," "*ten* men," "*a white* house."

A **pronoun** is a word used instead of a noun to prevent the too frequent repetition of the noun, as "John reads because *he* delights in study."

A **verb** is a word which signifies "to be," "to do," or "to suffer," and is used to affirm or ask questions, as "John *speaks*," "*Are* you ready?"

An **adverb** is a word which qualifies a verb, adjective, or other adverb, as "He reads *well*," "James is a *very* good boy," "Robert speaks *very* correctly."

A **preposition** connects words, and shows the relation between them, as "The dog is *under* the table," "My hat is *on* my head."

A **conjunction** connects words and sentences together, as "Call my brother *and* sister," "The pupils improve *because* they are studious."

An **interjection** is used to express some emotion of the mind in an emphatic or impressive manner, as "*Ah* me!" "*Oh* that men were wise!"

Exercise 3.

*Distinguish the different parts of speech :— *

Man, a, good, I, give, soon, on, and, oh! the, sun, while, him, break, where, about, because, alas! therefore, under, finely, teach, them, goodness, beautiful, army, an, hers, virtue, London, why, but, ten, adorn, beneath, by, indeed! truly, mankind, angelic, scratch, brush, paint, there, coming.

The man who reads the holy Bible learns from it to think and act aright; but, alas! many forget its teachings. .

---

* The first column of the Parsing Table, Appendix B., may be used at this stage.

THE ARTICLE.

An article is a word placed before a noun to limit its signification, as *a* man, *an* apple, *the* garden.

There are two articles, *a* or *an*, and *the*.

A or an is called the indefinite article, because it does not point out any particular object.

The is called the definite article, because it does point out some particular object.

A is used before a consonant, and before vowels having the power of a consonant, as *a* man, *a* union.

An is used before a vowel, silent h, and h aspirate when the accent falls on the second syllable of the word, as *an* eagle, *an* heir, *an* historical drama.

Exercise 4.

Supply suitable articles :—

Man,—ass,—house,—article,—desk,—turkey,— heir,—hospital,—pot,—book,— historical poem,— leaves,— romance,— apple,—pear,—unit,— hereditary,— pump,— eunuch,— ear,— treaties,— peaches,—accident.

THE NOUN.

A noun is the name of any living being, place, thing, or quality, as *John, angel, London, desk, truth.*

CLASSIFICATION.

Nouns are classed into *proper, common,* and *abstract.*

A proper noun is the name of a particular individual of a class or species, as *James, Dublin, Snowdon.*

When the proper noun is used as the type of a species it becomes common, as " He is the *Newton* of the age."

A common noun is the name applied to a whole class or species, as *man, city, mountain.*

Common nouns are sub-divided into *class, collective, concrete,* and *quantitative,* as *boy, crowd, silver, score.*

Abstract nouns express some quality, attribute, or state of an object.

They are subdivided into those of *quality, action, state;* and *verbal* nouns, as *sweetness, walk, sleep, talking.*[*]

---

[*] For a first course the primary classification may be deemed ~~dent.~~

Exercise 5.

Classify the following nouns :—

Robert, son, blackness, truth, woman, Charles, dog, holiness, Trusty, Thames, mountain, height, river, Snowdon, beauty, London, tree, stream, city, size, Paris, town, mob, gold, dozen, whiteness, walk, rest, hearing, village, army, Dudley, grass, race, iron, gross, grace, sleep, speaking, committee.

INFLECTION.

Inflection is a change in the form of a word, to express a difference of meaning, or relation to other words in the sentence.

Five parts of speech are inflected, the *noun, adjective, pronoun, verb,* and *adverb.*

Nouns are inflected to express *gender, number,* and *case.*

GENDER.

Gender is that inflection of the noun which indicates the sex of the object.

There are three genders, the *masculine, feminine,* and *neuter.*

The **masculine** gender of nouns denotes the male sex of animals, as *man, horse, bull.*

The **feminine** gender of nouns denotes the female sex of animals, as *woman, mare, cow.*

Nouns of the **neuter** gender denote that the things they represent are without life. The word *neuter* signifies neither, that is, neither male nor female.

When a noun may be applied to either sex it is said to be of the **common** gender, that is, common to both, as *child, parent, pupil, teacher,* &c.

Personification means the employment of words of the masculine or feminine gender to denote objects without life. For example, we sometimes speak of the sun as *he,* of the moon as *she,* &c.

Objects indicative of magnitude, strength, and courage are represented as masculine, as the *sun, death, winter time, anger, war,* &c.; those indicative of beauty, grace, gentleness, and fruitfulness are represented as feminine, as the *moon, ship, spring, hope, peace,* &c.

The gender of nouns is distinguished in three different ways :—

1. *By a different word; as,*

Bachelor	maid	Hound	brach
Beau	belle	Husband	wife
Boar	sow	King	queen
Boy	girl	Lord	lady
Brother	sister	Man	woman
Buck	doe	Master	mistress
Bull	cow	Milter	spawner
Bullock, ox, or } steer	heifer	Monk	nun
		Nephew	niece
Cock	hen	Papa	mamma
Colt	filly	Ram	ewe
Dog	bitch	Sir	madam
Drake	duck	Sloven	slut
Earl	countess	Son	daughter
Father	mother	Stag	hind
Friar	nun	Stallion	mare
Gander	goose	Swain	nymph
Gentleman	lady	Tutor	governess
Governor	matron	Uncle	aunt
Hart	roe	Wizard	witch
Horse	mare		

2. *By a different termination; as,*

Abbot	abbess	Jew	Jewess
Actor	actress	Lad	lass
Administrator	administratrix	Landgrave	landgravine
Adulterer	adulteress	Lion	lioness
Ambassador	embassadress	Marquis	marchioness
Arbiter	arbitress	Mayor	mayoress
Author	authoress	Murderer	murderess
Baron	baroness	Negro	negress
Benefactor	benefactress	Ogre	ogress
Bridegroom	bride	Patron	patroness
Caterer	cateress	Peer	peeress
Chanter	chantress	Poet	poetess
Conductor	conductress	Porter	portress
Count	countess	Priest	priestess
Czar	czarina	Prince	princess
Deacon	deaconess	Prior	prioress
Director	directress	Prophet	prophetess
Don	donna	Protector	protectress
Duke	duchess	Shepherd	shepherdess
Editor	editress	Signore	signora
Emperor	empress	Songster	songstress
Enchanter	enchantress	Sorcerer	sorceress
Executor	executrix	Sultan	sultaness, or sultana
Founder	foundress		
Giant	giantess	Testator	testatrix
Governor	governess	Tiger	tigress
Heir	heiress	Traitor	traitress
Hero	heroine	Tyrant	tyraness
Hunter	huntress	Viscount	viscountess

Host	hostess	Votary	votaress
Idolator	idolatress	Victor	victress
Infante	infanta	Widower	widow
Inventor	inventress		

3. *By joining masculine and femine terms; as,*

Man-servant	maid-servant	Cock-sparrow	hen-sparrow
Male child	female child	Billy-goat	nanny-goat
He-ass	she-ass	Peacock	pea-hen *
Bull-calf	cow-calf		

NUMBER.

Number is that inflection which shows whether one or more than one is meant.

There are two numbers, the *singular* and *plural*.

The **singular** denotes one, as *pen;* the plural more than one, as *pens.*

The **plural** is generally formed by adding *s* to the singular, as *book, books; tree, trees.*

Exceptions.

1. Nouns ending in *s, x, sh, ch* soft, or in *o* preceded by a conso-nant form the plural by adding *es,* as *glass, glasses; fox, foxes; fish, fishes; church, churches; hero, heroes.*
Junto, canto, grotto, tyro, portico, solo and *quarto,* together with those ending in *o* preceded by a vowel, add *s* only, as *junto, juntos; folio, folios.*
2. Nouns ending in *f* or *fe,* change *f* or *fe* into *ves,* as *loaf, loaves; life, lives.*
Chief, grief, dwarf, scarf, hoof, proof, gulf, turf, muff, stuff, sheriff, strife and a few others, add *s* only.
3. Nouns ending in *y,* preceded by a consonant, change *y* into *ies,* as *city, cities.*
Those ending in *y,* preceded by a vowel, add *s* only, *boy, boys.* .
4. The following form the plural irregularly:—

Man	men	Ox	oxen	Foot	feet
Woman	women	Mouse	mice	Tooth	teeth
Child	chidren	Louse	lice	Goose	geese

5. Some have two plurals:—

Brother	brothers, brethren	Fowl	fowl, fowls
Cannon	cannon, cannons	Genius	geniuses, genii
Cloth	cloths, clothes	Herring	herring, herrings
Cow	cows, kine	Index	indexes, indices
Die	dies, dice	Pea	peas, pease
Fish	fish, fishes	Penny	pennies, pence

6. Some nouns have the singular and plural alike, as—*brace, deer, dozen, grouse, salmon, series, sheep, swine, trout.*

---

* See Exercise 6, page 9.

7. The following have no plural:—
   a. Proper nouns, as *John, London, Thames.*
   b. Abstract nouns, generally, as *gentleness, truth, peace.*
   c. Names of metals, as *gold, iron, zinc.*
   d. Names of things weighed and measured, as *wheat, sugar, calico, tea, wine.* When different qualities or kinds are mentioned, these admit of a plural.
   e. Names of some arts and sciences, as *poetry, music, arithmetic.*

8. The following have no singular:—*ashes, annals, bellows, dress, entrails, lees, morals, nuptials, riches, scissors, snuffers, tidings, tongs, thanks, vitals, wages.*

9. Some are employed as singular or plural, as *amends, mathematics, means, odds, optics,* &c.

10. *Alms, gallows, news,* are generally singular.

11. Nouns adopted from foreign languages generally retain their original plurals.

Addendum	addenda	Genius	genii
Amanuensis	amanuenses	Hypothesis	hypotheses
Analysis	analyses	Index	indices
Apex	apices	Larva	larvæ
Appendix	appendices	Magus	magi
Animalculum	animalcula	Medium	media
Arcanum	arcana	Memorandum	memoranda
Axis	axes	Metamorphosis	metamorphoses
Bandit,banditto	bandits,banditti	Miasma	miasmata
Basis	bases	Monsieur	messieurs
Beau	beaux	Nebula	nebulæ
Cherub	cherubim	Oasis	oases
Crisis	crises	Parenthesis	parentheses
Criterion	criteria	Phasis	phases
Converzazione	converzazioni	Phenomenon	phenomena
Datum	data	Polypus	polypi
Desideratum	desiderata	Radius	radii
Dictum	dicta	Seraph	seraphim
Dilettante	dilettanti	Stimulus	stimuli
Effluvium	effluvia	Stratum	strata
Ellipsis	ellipses	Stamen	stamina
Emphasis	emphases	Terminus	termini
Erratum	errata	Thesis	theses
Focus	foci	Vertex	vertices
Formula	formulæ	Vortex	vortices
Fungus	fungi	Virtuoso	virtuosi
Genus	genera		

12. The following compound nouns, and others like them, form the plural as under:—
   Aid-de-camp   aids-de-camp.
   Court-martial   courts-martial.
   Cousin-german   cousins-german.
   Father-in-law   fathers-in-law.*

* See exercise 6, p. 9.

CASE.

Case is that inflection of the noun or pronoun which shows its relation to other words in the sentence.

There are three cases, the *nominative*, *possessive*, and *objective*, of which the nominative and objective of nouns are alike.

The **nominative** is the subject of the verb or affirmation, and is found in the sentence by asking the question " who ? " " which ? " or " what ? " as, " James sent the letter." " *Who* sent it ?" " James." *James*, therefore, is the nominative.

The **possessive** case implies ownership or possession. It is formed by adding an apostrophe and *s* to the nominative, as *brother*, *brother's*. It may be found by asking the question, " whose ?" as, " This is John's book." " Whose book ?" " John's." *John's* is therefore in the possessive.

The **objective** case expresses the object of the action, or some relation expressed by means of a preposition. It may be found by asking the question, " whom ?" " which ?" or " what ?" as, " Robert loves his brother." " *Whom* does he love ?" " His brother;" which words are therefore in the objective case.

Sometimes the objective with *of* takes the place of the possessive, as, " William's desk." " The desk of William."

When two possessives come together, one is expressed by means of a preposition, as, " John's brother's friend." " The friend of John's brother."

Plural nouns ending in *s*, and certain others, form the possessive by adding an apostrophe only, as, "The pupils' caps," "Moses' rod."

The noun is thus declined :—

	Sing.	Plural.	Sing.	Plural.
Nom.	Boy.	Boys.	Man.	Men.
Poss.	Boy's.	Boys'.	Man's.	Men's.
Obj.	Boy.	Boys.	Man.	Men.

Exercise 6.

Tell the gender, number, and case of the following nouns :—

Man, sister, book's, kings, lady, slate, gander, life, ewe, pig's, church, earls', seraph, drakes, deer, widow, fancy, harts, oxen sows', goose, Czarina, folios, flock, drakes', signore, odds, hinds brother, messieurs, village, gander, nymphs', pot, news, heroine duke's motto, parents', men, master's hat, sheep, fish's, fishes', mice, kinsman's tale, knives', tooth, beauties, swine, alms, calf's, amends, potatoes, brethren, shears, fowl, asses, grief, means, dies, chimneys, foxes'.

Exercise 7.

Supply suitable nouns.

The—barks,—talk, the—aches,—sing and play,—neigh,—bleat,—crows, the—is large, my—is small, the—squeaks, —proposes but—disposes,—chirp, a good—, a tall—,—mew, pretty—, heavenly—, rushing—, gladsome—, grand—, sublime—, magnificent—, the—plows the—, —peals the—, —'s — is lame, my — is old, the—speaks of —, — learns his — like a good —, a — of — knows the — of—, the — of the just is as the shining —, hear my — O —; give — unto my —, — and — I cry unto thee.

> For — and — to thee are one,
> The helpless are thy —;
> And for the — of thy dear —
> Thou hearst an —'s —.

The Song of Steam,
Harness me down with your iron —,
    Be sure of your — and —
For I scorn the — of your puny —,
    As the — scorns a —.
How I laughed as I lay concealed from—
    For many a countless —,
At the childish — of human —,
    And the — of human —.

THE ADJECTIVE.

An adjective is a word used to qualify a noun.

CLASSIFICATION.

Adjectives are classed into those of *quality, quantity,* and *distinction,* as "a *good* boy," "*ten* men," "a *monthly* periodical."

Adjectives of quantity refer both to quantity and number, and include the cardinal and ordinal numerals as "an *abundant* harvest," "*fifty* horses," "the *third* session."

The articles and demonstrative pronouns are sometimes treated as distinguishing adjectives.

INFLECTION.

The only inflection of which adjectives admit is, the *degrees of comparison,* which are three, the *positive, comparative,* and *superlative.*

The **positive** is the simple form of the adjective, and attributes some quality or circumstance to the noun without respect to any other, as " John is a *tall* boy."

The **comparative** expresses a higher degree of the quality expressed by the positive, as " John is *taller* than James."

The **superlative** expresses the highest degree of the quality expressed by the positive, as " John is the *tallest* boy in school."

The *comparative* is formed by adding r or *er* to the positive as *large, larger; great, greater.*

The *superlative* is formed by adding *st* or *est* to the positive as *large, largest; great, greatest.*

Adjectives of two or more syllables are generally compared by prefixing *more, most; less, least,* as " more useful," " less useful ;" " most useful," " least useful."

Obs. Strictly speaking the positive also expresses comparison, for we cannot say, " John is a *tall* boy " without indicating that he is tall as compared with others.

The following are irregularly compared :—

Pos.	Comp.	Sup.
Bad, evil, ill	worse	worst
(Beneath)	under	undermost
Down	......	......
Far	farther	farthest
Fore	former	foremost, first
(Forth)	further	furthest
Good	better	best
Head	......	headmost
Hind	hinder	hindmost, hindermost
(In)	inner	inmost, innermost
Late	later, latter	latest, last
Little	less	least
Low	lower	lowest, lowermost
Middle	......	middlemost
Much, many	more	most
(Neath)	nether	nethermost
Near, nigh	nearer	nearest, next
Old	older, elder	oldest, eldest
(Out)	outer	{ outmost, utmost, out-termost, uttermost
South	......	southmost
Top	......	topmost
Up	upper	upmost, uppermost
Very	......	veriest

Adjectives ending in *y* preceded by a consonant, change the *y* into *i* before *er* and *est*, as *lovely, lovelier, loveliest.*

Some double the final consonant before comparison, as *hot, hotter, hottest ; sad, sadder, saddest.*

Some adjectives, from their signification, do not admit of comparison, as *round, square, perfect, supreme, perpendicular, right, left, wrong, chief.*

The cardinal and ordinal adjectives of quantity are not compared, such as *four, fourth.*

Exercise 8.

Classify and compare (where possible) the following adjectives:—

Good, much, this, large, sweet, daily, supreme, excellent, green, round, truthful, tall, white, weekly, ten, that, short, low, bad, hot, right, magnanimous, near, violent, black, huge, thin, hard, slanting, crisp, luminous, haughty, rattling, triple, fourth, looming, fifty, abandoned, close, endearing, circular, rich, despised, late, up, wrong, iniquitous.

Exercise 9.

Supply suitable adjectives.

A—house,—men,— waistcoat,— coat,—serial,—bread,—boy,—girl, —tree,—stick,—speech,—landscape,—newspaper, the table is—, the field is—, the prospect is—, what a—sight!—times—make—11.0, there are—days in the—month, and—months in a year, sugar is —but vinegar is—, I play—violin in—style ; a—dog bit my—boy and made his—arm bleed in a—manner. The—density of—water as — with—water will decrease where the water is—and increase where it becomes—than the—average.

The wind disturbs the — lake,
And bids it ripple — and —.
It moves the — boughs till they make
— music in their — mesh.

There is a pleasure in the — woods,
There is a rapture on the — shore ;
There is society where — intrudes,
By the — sea and music in its roar.

THE PRONOUN.

A **pronoun** is a word used instead of a noun, to prevent the too frequent repetition of the noun, as " John reads because *he* likes study."

CLASSIFICATION.

Pronouns are of three kinds—*personal, relative,* and *adjective ;* and may be either *simple* or *compound.*

The *simple* **Personal** pronouns are *I, thou, he, she, it,* with their plurals, *we, you, they.*

I, the first personal pronoun, represents the speaker or actor.

Thou, the second, represents the person addressed.

He, she, or *it,* the third, represents the subject of discourse.

The **Relative** pronouns are *who, which, that,* and *what.* They are so called because they *relate* to some word or clause going before, which is called the *antecedent,* as " I esteem the boy *who* speaks the truth."

Obs.—Here *who* is the relative, and *boy* the antecedent.

Who is applied to persons only, as " The man *who* was here."

Which is applied to the lower animals and objects without life, as "The dog *which* barks," "The stone *which* fell."

That is applied to objects of every kind, as " The man *that* spoke," "The cat *that* mews," "The desk *that* was broken."

What is equivalent to both relative and antecedent, as " I reported *what* you said;" that is, " *that which* you said."

As, which is sometimes treated as a relative pronoun, must be employed with caution, and is chiefly used after *same,* as " He did the same as we anticipated."

Who, which, and what, when used to ask questions, are called interrogative pronouns.

The **Adjective** pronouns are so called because they partake both of the character of an adjective and pronoun.

They are of four kinds—*possessive, distributive, demonstrative,* and *indefinite.*

Possessive pronouns denote possession. They are, *my, thy, his, her, its, our, your their, own.*

The **Distributive** denote distribution or separation ; they are, *each, every, either, neither.*

The **Demonstrative** demonstrate or point out; they are, *this, that,* and in the plural, *these, those.*

The **Indefinite** pronouns are used in an indefinite or uncertain manner ; they are *some, any, one, all, such, other, another, both, none, several, certain, divers, same, whole.*

INFLECTION.

The **personal** pronouns are inflected by *gender, number,* and *case,* as follows :—

	1st. person—M. or F.		2nd. person—M. or F.	
	Sing.	**Plural**	**Sing.**	**Plural**
Nom.	I	we	thou	you
Poss.	mine	ours	thine	yours
Obj.	me	us	thee	you

C

| | 3rd person—M. F. N. | | M. F. N. |
	Sing.	Sing.	Sing.	Plural
Nom.	he	she	it	they
Poss.	his	hers	its	theirs
Obj.	him	her	it	them

The **relative** pronouns *who, which,* and *that,* are thus declined :—

	Sing. and Plural	Sing. and Plural	Singular.
Nom.	who	which	that
Poss.	whose	whose	...
Obj.	whom	which	that

The adjective pronouns *one, other, another,* are declined like nouns, with the exception of *another,* which has no plural.

COMPOUND PRONOUNS.

Compound pronouns are formed by the union of some other word with the simple pronouns.

The compound *personal* pronouns are, *myself, thyself, himself, herself, itself,* with their plurals, *ourselves, yourselves, themselves.* They are sometimes called the *emphatic* pronouns, because they add emphasis to the expression, and are the same in the nominative and objective cases, but have no possessive.

When the actor and the object of the action are the same, they are called *reflective,* as "He dresses *himself.*"

The compound *relative* pronouns besides *what,* are *whoever, whichever, whatever, whosoever whomsoever,* &c. They include both the relative and the antecedent, as "*Whoever* did that must suffer;" that is, "*He who* did that must suffer."

The compound *adjective* pronouns are *my own, thy own,* &c., and *each other, each the other, one another. My own, thy own,* &c., are the same in the nominative and objective, but have no possessive.

Each other, one another, are thus declined :—

	Singular	Singular
Nom.	each other	one another
Poss.	each other's	one another's
Obj.	each other	one another

Exercise 10.

Parse the following pronouns.

I, who, my, this, each, any, mine, whom, they, these, every, him, one, me, which, his, that, us, whatever, thine, either, they, all, it whom, she, such, her, those, thee, whomsoever, neither, hers, yours, such, itself, what, its, whichsoever, thou, some, those, he, ours, each other, ourselves, we, themselves.

Exercise 11.

Supply appropriate pronouns.

I love —, — hates —. He — is wicked, is not — friend. — cap fits —, — one fits — brother. — must bear — own burden. — is his — fault. — one may do —. — book is —. — is —. — are gone. Bring — — pens. The — — bought was —. Every — must do — duty. — knife have — found? My —. — intention is to excel —. — rule has — broken? —. Leave —. Take —. — do — mean? Have — seen — ? — do — mean? The man — stole — neighbour's horse. Let — man deem — unworthy of — reward. — course — may take will suit —. — have hurt — self.

Exercise 12

Supply appropriate articles, nouns, adjectives, and pronouns.

Value of Time.

Suffer — to impress upon — the — of — just — of —. Consider how much is to be performed, attained, and conquered, ere — are fitted to discharge (the) — — your — may comprehend. Think of (the) brevity of —. — most aged have compared—to a—in —, and to—shuttle in —. Compute — bearings upon the — or—of eternity, and remember if misspent, — can never be re-called.

The Verb.

A verb is a word which signifies "to be," "to do," or "to suffer," and is used to affirm or ask questions, as "John speaks," "*Are* you ready?"

CLASSIFICATION.

Verbs are of two kinds *transitive* and *intransitive*.

A **transitive** verb denotes that the action or emotion passes from the subject to some object, as "I *strike* the table."

Obs. Here the action *strike* passes from the subject *I* to the object *table.*

An **intransitive** verb denotes that the action or emotion is confined to the subject, as "I *sleep*," "I *run*."

c 2

Obs. The intransitive is sometimes followed by an object of similar meaning; or of distance, as "He slept *the sleep* of death," "He ran *a race*," "He walked *a mile*."

In respect of *formation*, verbs are also classed into *regular*, *irregular*, and *defective*.

A **regular** verb is one whose past tense and past participle are formed by the addition of *d* or *ed* as *love, loved; part, parted*.

An **irregular** verb is one whose past tense and past participle are formed in some other way, as *see, saw, seen; am, was, been*.

A **defective** verb is one deficient in some of its parts, as *may, shall, &c.*

Obs. Regular verbs are sometimes called *weak* verbs, because they require the addition of a suffix to form their past tense and past participle. Irregular are called *strong*, because they do not require this addition. Verbs possessing both forms are called *redundant*.

When one verb is used to *assist* another in the formation of its voices, moods, and tenses, it is called an *auxiliary* verb.

The **auxiliary** verbs are *be, have, do, shall, will, may, can, let, must, ought;* and are chiefly defective. *Be, have, do, will* are also used as principal verbs; the others are meaningless unless used with *principals*.

Verbs used only in the third person singular are called *impersonal*, as *it rains, it snows, it thunders*.

Classify the following verbs, (1) into transitive and intransitive, (2) into regular, irregular, and defective.

Love, speak, hurt, talk, may, come, strike, tumble, hear, do, break, strew, fall, pity, know, attend, will, make, sail, read, reach, ride, touch, rise, proceed, shall, shine, merit, show, preserve, smite, am, bestow, ring, can, complain, think, permit, must, stand, assert, thrive, approach, play, thrust, work, establish, write, estimate wake.

INFLECTION.

Verbs are inflected to express *voice, mood, tense, number,* and *person*.

VOICE.

Transitive verbs have two voices, the *active* and *passive*.

The **active** voice denotes that the subject acts, as "James *loves*."

The **passive** voice denotes that the subject is acted

upon, or is the object of the action or emotion, as "James *is loved* by John."

MOOD.

Mood is that inflection of a verb which indicates the *mode*, or *condition*, of an action.

Verbs have five moods, the *indicative, subjunctive, potential, imperative*, and *infinitive*.

The **indicative** asserts or indicates, as "I love."

The **subjunctive** implies condition or contingency, and is expressed by means of a conjunction, as *if, though, unless, except, till, until, lest*, as "If I come," "Though he slay me." It is used only in subordinate sentences.

The **potential** implies power, will, or obligation, as "I can love," "I would run," "He must go."

The **imperative** commands, exhorts, or entreats, as "Leave me," "Do learn your lesson."

The **infinitive** expresses action generally, without reference to any subject, as "To love."

A **participle** is so called because it partakes of the character of a verb, adjective, and noun. When used as an adjective it admits of comparison, as "*A more imposing* sight has seldom been witnessed."

TENSE.

The **tense** of a verb refers to the *time* of the action. There are, strictly speaking, only three tenses referring to action, *present, past*, or *future*; but, in order more clearly to define the particular time of the action the *perfect, pluperfect*, and *future-perfect* are added. These may respectively be considered as *primary* and *secondary* tenses.

Obs. The present and past tenses, indicative and subjunctive, alone are expressed by means of the inflected principal verb; the others are formed by means of auxiliaries.

NUMBER.

Verbs have two **numbers** the *singular* and *plural*, as "He loves," "They love."

PERSON.

Verbs have three **persons**, the *first, second*, and *third*, as "I speak," "Thou speakest," "He speaks."

Conjugation means the arrangement of a verb into its various voices, moods, tenses, numbers, and persons. The conjugating of a verb sometimes refers to the repetition of its three chief parts, the present, past, and past participle.

DEFECTIVE VERBS.

Present.	Past.	Past Participle.	Infinitive.
Beware	...	...	to beware
Can	could	...	...
Forego	...	foregone	to forego
May	might	...	...
Must	...	...	...
Ought	ought	...	...
Quoth	quoth	...	...
Shall	should	...	...
Wis	wist	...	...
Wit, or wot	wot	...	to wit

TO LOVE.

ACTIVE VOICE.

Present Indicative.	Past Indicative.	Past Participle.
Love.	Loved.	Loved.

INDICATIVE MOOD.   SUBJUNCTIVE MOOD.

Present Tense.

Singular—
1. I love
2. Thou lovest
3. He loves

Plural—
1. We love
2. You love
3. They love

Singular—
1. (If) I love
2. (If) thou love
3. (If) he love

Plural—
1. (If) we love
2. (If) you love
3. (If) they love

Past.

Singular—
1. I loved
2. Thou lovedst
3. He loved

Plural—
1. We loved
2. You loved
3. They loved

Singular—
1. (If) I loved
2. (If) thou lovedst
3. (If) he loved

Plural—
1. (If) we loved
2. (If) you loved
3. (If) they loved

Future.

Singular—
1. I shall love
2. Thou wilt love
3. He will love

Plural—
1. We shall love
2. You will love
3. They will love

Singular—
1. (If) I should love
2. (If) thou shouldst love
3. (If) he should love

Plural—
1. (If) we should love
2. (If) you should love
3. (If) they should love

Perfect.

Singular—
1. I have loved
2. Thou hast loved
3. He has loved

Plural—
1. We have loved
2. You have loved
3. They have loved

Singular—
1. (If) I have loved
2. (If) thou hast loved
3. (If) he has loved

Plural—
1. (If) we have loved
2. (If) you have loved
3. (If) they have loved

Pluperfect.

Singular—
1. I had loved
2. Thou hadst loved
3. He had loved

Plural—
1. We had loved
2. You had loved
3. They had loved

Singular—
1. (If) I had loved
2. (If) thou hadst loved
3. (If) he had loved

Plural—
1. (If) we had loved
2. (If) you had loved
3. (If) they had loved

Future Perfect.

Singular—
1. I shall have loved
2. Thou wilt have loved
3. He will have loved

Plural—
1. We shall have loved
2. Thou will have loved
3. They will have loved

Singular—
1. (If) I shall have loved
2. (If) thou wilt have loved
3. (If) he will have loved

Plural—
1. (If) he shall have loved
2. (If) you will have loved
3. (If) they will have loved

POTENTIAL MOOD.

Present Tense.

Singular—
1. I may, can, or must love
2. Thou mayst, canst, or must love
3. He may, can, or must love

Plural—
1. We may, can, or must love
2. You may, can, or must love
3. They may, can, or must love

Perfect.

Singular—
1. I may, can, or must have loved
2. Thou mayst, &c., have loved
3. He may, &c., have loved

Plural—
1. We may, &c., have loved
2. You may, &c., have loved
3. They may, &c., have loved

POTENTIAL MOOD.

Past.	Pluperfect.
Singular—	*Singular—*
1. I might, could, would, or should love	1. I might, could, would, or should have loved
2. Though mightst, &c., love	2. Thou mightest, &c., have loved
3. He might, &c., love	3. He might, &c., have loved
Plural—	*Plural—*
1. We might, &c., love	1. We might, &c., have loved
2. You might, &c., love	2. You might, &c., have loved
3. They might, &c., love	3. They might, &c., have loved

IMPERATIVE MOOD.

Present.

Singular—	*Plural—*
2. Love, or love thou	2. Love, or love ye

Future.

2. Thou shalt love	2. You shall love
3. He shall love	3. They shall love

INFINITIVE MOOD.

Present—To love	Perfect—To have loved

PARTICIPLE.

Present—Loving	Past—Loved	Perfect — Having loved

PROGRESSIVE FORM.

INDICATIVE.	SUBJUNCTIVE.	POTENTIAL.
Present—I am loving, &c.	(If) I be loving, &c.	I may, can, or must be loving, &c.

IMPERATIVE.

Present—Be thou loving, &c.	Future—Thou shalt be loving, &c.

INFINITIVE.

Present—To be loving.	Perfect—To have been loving.

PARTICIPLE.

Present — Being loving	Past—Been loving	Perfect — Having been loving

When the auxiliary verb *do* is used in the present and past indicative either affirmatively or interrogatively, it is called the *Emphatic Form*.

Affirmative.	Interrogative.
Present—I do call, &c.	*Present*—Do I call? &c.
*—*I did call, &c.	*Past*—Did I call? &c.

PASSIVE VOICE.

The passive voice is formed of the verb " to be," and the past participle of the principal verb.*

INDICATIVE.	SUBJUNCTIVE.	PAST PARTICIPLE.

Present Tense.

Singular—	Singular—	
1. I am	1. (If) I be	loved
2. Thou art	2. (If) thou be	,,
3. He is	3. (If) he be	,,
Plural—	Plural—	
1. We are	1. (If) we be	,,
2. You are	2. (If) you be	,,
3. They are	3. (If) they be	,,

Past.

Singular—	Singular—	
1. I was	1. (If) I were	loved
2. Thou wast	2. (If) thou wert	,,
3. He was	3. (If) he were	,,
Plural—	Plural—	
1. We were	1. (If) we were	,,
2. You were	2. (If) you were	,,
3. They were	3. (If) they were	,,

Future.

Singular—	Singular—	
1. I shall be	1. (If) I should be	loved
2. Thou wilt be	2. (If) thou shouldst be	
3. He will be	3. (If) he should be	,,
Plural—	Plural—	,,
1. We shall be	1. (If) we should be	,,
2. You will be	2. (If) you should be	,,
3. They will be	3. (If) they should be	,,

Perfect.

Singular—	Singular—	
1. I have been	1. (If) I have been	loved
2. Thou hast been	2. (If) thou hast been	,,
3. He has been	3. (If) he has been	,,
Plural—	Plural—	
1. We have been	1. (If) we have been	,,
2. You have been	2. (If) you have been	,,
3. They have been	3. (If) they have been	,,

---

* The teacher will find it convenient to teach the verb " to be " by itself first.

Pluperfect.

Singular—
1. I had been
2. Thou hadst been
3. He had been

Plural—
1. We had been
2. You had been
3. They had been

Singular—
1. (If) I had been   loved
2. (If) thou hadst been   "
3. (If) he had been   "

Plural—
1. (If) we had been   "
2. (If) you had been   "
3. (If) they had been   "

Future Perfect.

Singular—
1. I shall have been
2. Thou wilt have been
3. He will have been

Plural—
1. We shall have been
2. You will have been
3. They will have been

Singular—
1. (If) I shall have been   loved
2. (If) thou wilt have been
3. (If) he will have been   "

Plural—
1. (If) we shall have been   "
2. (If) you will have been   "
3. (If) they will have been   "

POTENTIAL MOOD.

Present Tense.

Singular—
1. I may, can, or must be
2. Thou mayst, &c., be
3. He may, &c., be

Plural—
1. We may, &c., be
2. Thou may, &c., be
3. They may, &c., be

Perfect.

Singular—
1. I may, can, or must have been   loved
2. Thou mayst, &c., have been   "
3. He may, &c., have been   "

Plural—
1. We may, &c., have been   "
2. You may, &c., have been   "
2. They may, &c., have been   "

Past.

Singular—
1. I might, could, would, or should be
2. Thou might, &c., be
3. He might, &c., be

Plural—
1. We might, &c., be
    You might, &c., be
    they might, &c., be

Pluperfect.

Singular—
1. I might, could, would, or should have been   loved
2. Thou mightest &c., have been   "
3. He might, &c., have been   "

Plural—
1. We might, &c., have been   "
2. You might, &c., have been   "
3. They might, &c., have been   "

IMPERATIVE MOOD.

Present.

Singular—		Plural—	
2. Be, or be thou		2. Be, or be ye	loved

Future.

2. Thou shalt be		2. You shall be	,,
3. He shall be		3. They shall be	,,

INFINITIVE MOOD.

Present—To be	} Perfect—To have been	,,

PARTICIPLE.

Perfect—Being	Past—Been	Perfect — Having been loved.

PROGRESSIVE FORM.

INDICATIVE.	SUBJUNCTIVE.	POTENTIAL.	
Present—I am being, &c.,	none	none	loved
Past—I was being, &c.,	none	none	,,

The rest are wanting in the passive voice. The emphatic form is also wanting in the passive voice.

Remarks.

The very name of the verb (VERBUM, a word) indicates its prominence in language. It is the most important part of speech, and the most difficult to be thoroughly learned, in any language, from its varied uses, classifications, and inflections.

The modern tendency of the English and most other modern languages is, to drop inflection. The form hath, loveth, &c., for the third person singular, is now seldom used, except in poetry. The form thou of the pronoun is used chiefly in addressing the Supreme Being and in poetry, you being employed instead. Ye is used in the imperative mood, and seldom elsewhere.

The past participle, and not the past tense, must be used after the auxiliaries be and have, as "I have written," not, "I have wrote." A good method therefore of finding the past participle of a verb is to use either of these first; thus, "I have — spoken."

After the verbs bid, dare, need, and some others, the preposition to is omitted before the infinitive, as "I need not (to) tell you."

Some verbs undergo change during inflection, as try, tryest, tries; let, lettest; die, dying.

Some grammarians would abolish inflection entirely in the subjunctive mood. When doubt and futurity are both implied, this mood should be used, as "If thou love," which is in fact equivalent to "If thou shouldst love." The distinction, however, is not always observed, even by distinguished writers.

"To express simple futurity, shall is used in the first person, and will in the second and third; as I shall come, thou wilt come, he will *come. Will*, in the first person, generally denotes determination: as *I will come*; and *shall*, in the second and third persons, generally denote authority: *Thou shalt not kill; he shall come to-morrow." Morell's Grammar*, p. 41.

Exercise 14.

Tell the person, number, tense, mood, and voice of the following verbs :—

I am. We love. I was walking. I am struck. To speak. Love thou. I do speak. Thou hatest. He had been loving. Thou wast heard. To be struck. Be thou persuaded. Thou didst hear. You laugh. He has been paying. He sits. He has been rejected. To have seen. We had been playing. They learn. I struck. Though they call. We shall be roaming. They will pity. Thou hast cut. We had been proposed. To have been dressed. You will be seeing. Standing. You have spoiled. You will be approved. Being touched. They might have been singing. We had spoken. They will have been struck. Broken. She will teach. I may be despised. John does good. Thou wilt prosper. I may try. Thou mightst be injured. Being dropped. Flee ye. James did tell. We might have waited. Having cast. They are loving. John might have been killed. Thou mightst fall. Having been caught. If I were seen. You have been praying. You may have failed. If I come. Thomas is teaching. Escape. We shall have been thinking. If thou be right. William taught. Run. The man had been working. Though thou hadst been killed. Be ye washed. To have loved. If we shall have been prevented. Having been punished.

Exercise 15.

Supply appropriate verbs.

Birds —. Dogs —. Horses —. Serpents —. I —. Thou —. He —. Cattle —. The hen —. The wolf—. Cats—. Pigeons—. The sparrow —. We are —. Pupils — their lessons. Men — wages. The people — their rulers. He — a slate and then — it. He was — to — for the injury he had —. John has — a long letter and — it by post. He — a valuable service and was—by ingratitude. The poor — often more — than the rich. The glass was — by — on the floor. The rain has — the rivers and the country is—. We — the eloquence of Cicero and — his patriotism. Inquests on the bodies of persons — by railway accidents usually — in — us little but what — well—before. A coroner's duty — simply that of—into the cause of death. It — no part of his business to — an investigation with the view of — a system of management, or of — the recurrence of accidents.

IRREGULAR VERBS.

Irregular Verbs are divided into three classes :—

1. Those which have only one form for the present tense, past tense, and past participle.

2. Those which have two forms for these parts.

3. Those which have three forms for these parts.

CLASS 1.

Bet, hunt, cast, cost, cut, hit, hurt, knit, let, put, read, rid, set, shed, shred, shut, slit, split, spread, sweat, thrust, wed, wet.

CLASS 2.

Present.	Past.	Past participle.	Present.	Past.	Past participle.
Abide	abode	abode	*Light	lit	lit
*Awake	awoke	awoke	Lose	lost	lost
Beat	beat	beaten	Make	made	made
Behold	beheld	beheld	Mean	meant	meant
Bend	bent	bent	Meet	met	met
*Bereave	bereft	bereft	Pay	paid	paid
Beseech	besought	besought	*Reave	reft	reft
Bind	bound	bound	Rend	rent	rent
Bleed	bled	bled	Run	ran	run
*Blend	blent	blent	Say	said	said
Breed	bred	bred	Seek	sought	sought
Bring	brought	brought	Sell	sold	sold
Build	built	built	Send	sent	sent
*Burn	burnt	burnt	Shine	shone	shone
Buy	bought	bought	Shoe	shod	shod
Catch	caught	caught	Shoot	shot	shot
Cling	clung	clung	Sit	sat	sat
*Clothe	clad	clad	Sleep	slept	slept
Come	came	come	Slide	slid	slid
Creep	crept	crept	Sling	slung	slung
Deal	dealt	dealt	Slink	slunk	slunk
Dig	dug	dug	Smell	smelt	smelt
*Dream	dreamt	dreamt	*Speed	sped	sped
Dwell	dwelt	dwelt	Spend	spent	spent
Feed	fed	fed	Spill	spilt	spilt
Feel	felt	felt	Spin	spun	spun
Fight	fought	fought	Stand	stood	stood
Find	found	found	Stave	stove	stove
Flee	fled	fled	Stick	stuck	stuck
Fling	flung	flung	Sting	stung	stung
Gild	gilt	gilt	Strike	struck	struck
Gird	girt	girt	String	strung	strung
Grind	ground	ground	Sweep	swept	swept
*Hang	hung	hung	Swing	swung	swung
Have	had	had	Teach	taught	taught
Hear	heard	heard	Tell	told	told
Hold	held	held	Think	thought	thought
Keep	kept	kept	*Wake	woke	woke
*Kneel	knelt	knelt	Weep	wept	wept
Lay	laid	laid	Win	won	won
Lead	led	led	Wind	wound	wound
*Leap	leapt	leapt	*Work	wrought	wrought
Leave	left	left	Wring	wrung	wrung
Lend	lent	lent			

* Those marked with an asterisk are redundant.

D

CLASS 3.

Present.	Past.	Past participle.	Present.	Past.	Past participle.
Am	was	been	See	saw	seen
Arise	arose	arisen	Seethe	seethed	sodden
Bear (to give birth)	bore, bare	born	Sew	sewed	sewn
			Shake	shook	shaken
Bear (to carry)	bore	borne	*Shave	shaved	shaven
			Shear	shore	shorn
Begin	began, begun	begun	Shew	shewed	shewn
			Show	showed	shown
Bid	bade	bidden, bid	Shrink	shrank, shrunk	shrunk, shrunken
Bite	bit	bitten, bit			
Blow	blew	blown	Shrive	shrove, shrived	shriven
Break	broke	broken			
Chide	chid	chidden, chid	Sing	sang, sung	sung
			Sink	sank, sunk	sunk
Choose	chose	chosen	Slay	slew	slain
Cleave (to split)	cleft	cleft, cleaved	Slink	slank, slunk	slunk
Crow	crew	crowed	Smite	smote	smitten, smit
Dare, durst	durst	dared			
			Sow	sowed	sown
Do	did	done	Speak	spoke	spoken, spoke
Draw	drew	drawn			
Dress	dressed	drest	Spin	span, spun	spun
Drink	drank	drunk	Spit	spat, spit	spitten, spit
Drive	drove	driven			
Eat	ate	eaten	Spring	sprang, sprung	sprung
Fall	fell	fallen			
Fly	flew	flown	Steal	stole	stolen
Forsake	forsook	forsaken	Straw	strawed	strawn
Freeze	froze	frozen	Stink	stank, stunk	stunk
Get	got	gotten, got			
Give	gave	given	Stride	strode	stridden
Go	went	gone	Strive	strove	striven
Grave	graved	graven	Strew	strewed	strewn
Grow	grew	grown	Strow	strowed	strown
Hew	hewed	hewn	Swear	swore	sworn
Hide	hid	hidden, hid	Swell	swelled	swollen
Hold	held	holden, held	Swim	swam	swum
			Take	took	taken
Know	knew	known	Tear	tore	torn
Lade	laded	laden	Thrive	throve	thriven
Lie	lay	lain	Throw	threw	thrown
Mow	mowed	mown	Tread	trod	trodden, trod
Ride	rode	ridden, rode			
			Wax	waxed	waxen
			Wear	wore	worn
Ring	rang, rung	rung	Weave	wove	woven
Rise	rose	risen	Write	wrote	written
Rive	rived	riven			
Saw	sawed	sawn			

Exercise 16.

Give (1) the past tense and past participle of the following verbs, and (2) point out the redundant verbs:—

Bet, abide, am, burst, awake, arise, cast, beat, bear, cost, bend, bid, bind, bite, bleed, blow, cut, build, blend, knit, burn, chide, cling, crow, do, dare, set, clothe, draw, shut, dig, drink, fly, thrust, dream, get, grave, split, spit, flee, grind, hew, lade, ring, seethe, wed, slink, speed, saw, shave, sing, met, hang, hide, kneel, know, leap, light, lie, lose, reave, see, shoe, spend, rive, sow, teach, swell, wake, thrive, win, wax, work, wear, wring, write.

THE ADVERB.

An **adverb** is a word which qualifies a verb, adjective, or other adverb, as " he reads *well*," " James is a *very* good boy," " Robert speaks *very* correctly."

CLASSIFICATION.

Adverbs may be divided into eight classes—

1. *Time,*—Now, then, lately, soon, &c.
2. *Place,*—Here, there, where, afar, whence, &c.
3. *Manner,*—Well, ill, thus, badly, &c.
4. *Cause and effect,*—Hence, therefore, since, because, &c.
5. *Number,*—Once, twice, thrice, often, &c.
6. *Order,*—Firstly, secondly, thirdly, lastly, &c.
7. *Affirmation and negation,*—Yes, yea, aye, no, not, &c.
8. *Quantity and degree,*—Much, nearly, enough, quite, &c.

Some adverbs are used to ask questions and are then called interrogative adverbs, as *where, when, how, why, whence,* &c.

Adverbs derived from the relative pronouns and some others, such as *while, where, whether, whence, why, how, after,* &c., serve to relate the different clauses of a sentence, and are then called *relative adverbs,* as " we found him *where* we left him." When so used they are sometimes denominated *adverbial conjunctions.*

When several words are used together, having the power of an adverb, they are called an *adverbial phrase,* as *by and bye, here and there, now and then, at last, to and fro, in truth,* &c.

Obs.—The same words are frequently used as adverbs, prepositions, and conjunctions, and the sense of the sentence must determine to which class of words they belong.

Some adverbs are the same as their relative adjectives, as *loud, hard, fast, quick, much, ill,* &c.

INFLECTION.

Some adverbs, like adjectives, admit of inflection according to the degrees of comparison, as—

Soon, sooner, soonest.
Often, oftener, oftenest.
Much, more, most.
Well, better, best.
Ill, worse, worst.
Sweetly, more sweetly, most sweetly.

Exercise 17.

Point out the adverbs and state what they qualify.

Come here. I will not. Are you there? Yes. How often did you fall? Never. I like it much. I had almost fallen. Very well. He is badly taught. He threw twice. You are almost dead with fright. They acted quickly and wisely. Snowdon is very high. Be off. Look up. He speaks very foolishly. Why do you stay here? Go on. The sea is exceedingly deep. The water is quite frozen over, and the fishes are almost benumbed.

Exercise 18.

Supply appropriate adverbs.

Look —. Run —. — long have you been — ? — a month. You speak —. Have you -- seen my brother? That book is — torn, it has been — used. — shall we hear the trumpet sound? Go —. John, — are you? I am —. The banner floats —. Will you return —? I will return — I can. Do you speak — ? —. You are — patient, — you shall be — rewarded.

Exercise 19.

Classify the following adverbs.

Once, now, well, yes, much, firstly, here, hence nearly, twice, aye, ill, lately, thirdly, wherefore, where, soon, thrice, no, gently, presently, thrice, enough, since, afar, not, then, quite, consequently, everywhere, fifthly, only, notwithstanding, however, fast, truly, indeed, up, well, loud, again, seldom.

THE PREPOSITION.

A preposition connects words and shows the relation between them, as "the dog is *under* the table." It is so called because it is *generally* placed before the word it governs.

The principal relations expressed by prepositions are those of *place, time, cause,* and *instrument,* as—

1. My hat is *on* the table.

2. He came *after* me.
3. He did it *through* ignorance.
4. John was struck *with* a stone.

Prepositions may relate nouns or pronouns, (1) to *other nouns or pronouns*, (2) to *verbs*, (3) to *adjectives*, as—

1. To another noun   A *man* of *understanding*.
2. To a verb   He *acts* with *prudence*.
3. To an adjective   It is *agreeable to him*.

List of Prepositions.

Abaft	athwart	down	off	touching
about	before	during	on	toward
above	behind	except	over	towards
across	below	excepting	regarding	under
after	beneath	for	respecting	underneath
against	beside	from	round	until
along	besides	in	save	unto
amid	between	into	since	up
amidst	betwixt	near	through	upon
among	beyond	next	throughout	with
amongst	but	nigh	till	within
around	by	of	to	without
at	concerning			

Of these *save, except, concerning, during, regarding, respecting,* and *touching*, are derived from verbs, and *near, next, nigh*, from adjectives.

Several are also used as adverbs, the context alone distinguishing them. When prepositions, a noun or pronoun, expressed or understood, comes before or after.

When two or more words coming together have the power of a preposition, they form *prepositional phrases*, as *according to, on account of, for the sake of, by means of*, &c.

Prepositions frequently unite with verbs, forming *compound verbs*, as *go, undergo ; look, overlook*, &c.

Exercise 20.

Point out, (1) *the prepositions*, (2) *the words they govern, and* (3) *the words they relate.*

He is of age. Put the pen on the desk. He walks round the table. He acted in haste, according to his custom. Sit beside me and keep still for an hour. John walked across the street and fell against a wall. During a cold evening in December my brother and I set off on a journey of adventure, which lasted throughout the winter, and was productive both of amusement and instruction, which, during the following season, we undertook to communicate to others. Almost up to the close of the last parliamentary session, the press duly, for the space of about two years, kept the public informed of the meetings of the Royal Commission of Inquiry into Primary Education, Ireland.

Exercise 21.

Supply appropriate prepositions.

He lives — London. An act — Parliament. He acts — reason. Walk — the garden. Sit — your place. Read — care. He fell — the wall. Walk — with him and let the others come — you. He lives — the bounties — the land, and looks — the miseries — others — indifference. — a series — criminal enterprises, the liberties — Europe have been gradually extinguished; and we are the only people — the eastern hemisphere who are — possession — equal laws and a free constitution.

> Sweet was the sound when oft — evening's close,
> — yonder hill the village murmur rose;
> There, as I passed — careless steps and slow,
> The mingling notes came softened — below.

THE CONJUNCTION.

The **conjunction** connects words and sentences, as " Call my brother *and* sister," "The pupils improve *because* they are studious."

Obs.—Although in the first example the *and* connects words, it in reality connects sentences, for the expression is equivalent to "call my brother and (call my) sister."

CLASSIFICATION.

Conjunctions are classed into *co-ordinate* and *subordinate*.

Co-ordinate conjunctions connect sentences of equal rank or value, and which are independent of each other, as—

" William invaded England and defeated Harold."

Subordinate conjunctions connect sentences some of which are dependent on another, as—

" I will leave you, *since* you desire it."

Obs.—The latter clause here being dependent on the former, it is connected by a subordinate conjunction.

Co-ordinate Conjunctions.

Accordingly	else	moreover	or
And	for	nevertheless	otherwise
Also	further	nor	still
Both	hence	neither [ing	therefore
But	however	notwithstand-	whence
Consequently	indeed	now	wherefore
Either	likewise	only	yet

Subordinate Conjunctions.

After	how	since	whence
Although	however	that	where
As	if	than	wherein
Because	lest	though	whereon
Before	notwithstand-	until	while
Ere	ing	unless	whither
Except	provided	when	why
For			

Some conjunctions require others after them, as—

As—so	for—because	not only—but	though—yet
Both—and	if—then	so—as	though—still
Either—or	neither—nor	so—that	whether—or

Conjunctional phrases.—*As well as, as soon as, in as far as, in as much as, after that, as often as, as long as, now that, so that, &c.*

Exercise 22.

Point out and classify the conjunctions.

He and I. Both Tom and Robert. They left because it was late. Neither you nor your brother was there. I will stay until you come. I worked, otherwise I should have starved. He reads that he may learn. He and his brother must succeed, for they are always studying. If you disregard our request yet we will persist. Although the time is short yet you may make up for that by diligence and attention.

THE INTERJECTION.

The interjection is used to express some emotion of the mind in an abrupt or emphatic manner, as "*Ah me!*" "*Oh that men were wise!*"

The interjection may frequently be omitted without injuring the sense of the sentence, hence its name.

The interjections are—

Ah!	faugh!	ho!	hurrah! oho!
Ay, ay!	fie!	hallo!	O!
Bravo!	heigh-ho!	hist!	Oh!

Other parts of speech, when used in an abrupt manner, have the power of interjections, as *hush! hark! behold! hold! indeed! truly! strange! welcome! adieu! gracious! yes! no! well!*

Exercise 22.

Point out the adverbs, prepositions, conjunctions, and interjections.

Look out. Sit on your seat. Come and see. Yes, you promised well, but alack! where is the fulfilment of your promise? How admirably she sings! It remains for you to decide quickly as to our course of action. Oh! that I had listened sooner to your advice, and had not followed evil counsel! When do you intend to visit and condole with your bereaved friend? I there and then resolved to pursue the path of duty as dictated by my own convictions, for I had already proved his advice to be worthless; and but for this timely determination should have had—too late, perhaps—to mourn over a lost opportunity.

Remarks.

Many words in English, spelt alike, are used as different parts of speech, and the only guide to the proper parsing of such is the meaning or context of the sentence. The English language, too, is so little inflected as compared with ancient and most other modern languages, that the meaning alone must determine the parts of speech to which they belong. Thus, *love, talk, present, light,* &c., are used as verbs and nouns, *light* and *present* being also used as adjectives. *As* is used as an adverb and conjunction; *but* as an adverb, preposition, and conjunction; *for* as a conjunction and preposition; *no* as an adjective and adverb; *one, other,* and *another* each as a noun, pronoun, and adjective; *only* as an adjective and adverb; *save* as an adverb and preposition; *since* as an adverb, preposition, and conjunction; *that* as a relative and adjective pronoun, and as a conjunction. *Much, more,* and *most,* when qualifying nouns, are adjectives——when qualifying adjectives, adverbs; *while, well, till, down, round, like,* and some others are also variously used.

Exercise 24.

Parse the words in italics according to columns 1, 2, 3, 4, 5, 6 of Parsing Table, Appendix B.

Love is the fulfilling of the law. *Love* your enemies. He is wise who *talks* little. The *talk* of the company was chiefly on politics. The master *presents* the successful pupils with *presents,* the whole school being *present.* *One* man loves what *another* despises. Choose this *one* and I will purchase *another.* *While* the grass grows. Wait a *while.* Wait *till* I come and then begin to *till* the garden. *Well,* my boy, how are you? Very *well.* His tears *well* from their fountains. *Still* evening approaches. Bid him *still* the horses. *Still* will I try the last. He fell *down.* He ran *down* the road. *Down* is very soft. Is this the *down* train? No, it is the *up* one. Look *up.* Walk *round* the table and sing a *round.* The wheel goes *round.* Where will you find their *like* again? *Like* as a father pitieth his children. I *like* not his dealings. *Light* the candle and give us *light,* and take that *light* chair away. *As* he was going away we gave him as good advice *as* possible. None but the deserving were recognised. I will go, *but* you must stay. There are *but* two here. Did no one attend? *No,* many attended. The *only* *one* who escaped said there were *only* four left. I think *that* you should consider *that* man a friend *that* is always ready to help you. I say *that that* *that that* man wrote is well written. *Much* good might be done if *more* would unite, as *most* good is done by united action. He was *much* improved, and therefore *more* capable of accomplishing what is really a *most* difficult undertaking. Let us *save* ourselves by flight, for none *save* the active can escape. *Since* you ask me I will do it, for it is long *since* I met such a friend.

CHAPTER III.

SYNTAX.

Syntax is that part of grammar which treats of the connection and arrangement of words in sentences.

It consists of two parts, *concord* and *government.*

Concord means the agreement of one word with another in *gender, number, case,* or *person.*

Government means the ruling of one word by another in a particular *case* or *mood.*

A sentence is a complete thought expressed in language.

Sentences are either *simple, complex,* or *compound.*

A simple sentence contains but one subject or nominative, and one finite verb,* as "John speaks."

A complex sentence contains one principal clause and one or more subordinate clauses, as "John laughs because his brother cries."

A compound sentence contains two or more simple or complex sentences expressing thoughts independent of each other, as "John laughs at his brother, and causes him to be angry."

RULES OF SYNTAX.

CONCORD.

Rule I. An adjective agrees with its noun in gender, number, and case, as "A good boy," "A modest girl," "This pen," "These apples."

Note 1. This and *that* are the only adjectives *inflected* to agree with their nouns; all other adjectives, although unchanged in form, are said to agree with the nouns they qualify, in "gender, number, and case."

Note 2. In composition *this* and *these* refer to the *latter; that* and

---

* Any part of a verb is called *finite* which is not limited by person or number, that is, every part except the participles and infinitive.

those to the *former* as "Virtue and vice alike prevail, *this* degrades man, *that* ennobles him; the *former* leads to happiness, the *latter* to misery." The *one*, the *other*, are similarly applied to the *former*, *latter*, but the distinction is not always observed, even by good writers.

RULE II. Nouns signifying the same thing agree in case as "*Canning the statesman.*"

Note 1. Such nouns are said to be in apposition and may either precede the verb or be before and after it, as "*Macaulay* the *historian* wrote essays," "*Macaulay* was an *historian.*"

RULE III. A verb agrees with its nominative in number and person, as "I read," "Thou readest," "He reads."

Note 1. The infinitive mood or part of a sentence is also used as a nominative, as "*To ride* is pleasant," "*To speak the truth* is commendable."

Note 2. The nominative generally precedes the verb. The chief exceptions are in interrogatory and emphatic sentences, and in poetry, as "Have you seen him?" "Attend ye to instruction." "Full knee-deep lies the winter snow."

RULE IV. The verb *to be* and some others, take the same case after as before them, as "*I* am *he*," "*Thou* art named John," "*He* acts as a *statesman.*"

Note 1. In such cases the words are in apposition, this being in fact another form of Note 1, Rule II.

RULE V. The relative pronoun agrees with its antecedent in gender, number, and person, as "The man who speaks,' "The stone which fell," "Thou who hast spoken."

Note 1. The antecedent may be a sentence or part of a sentence, "He injured his foot, which caused him much pain."

Note 2. Collective nouns when treated as singular are followed by the relative *which;* when plural, the relative must agree with the *individuals* represented by the collective noun.

Note 3. The antecedent *generally* precedes the relative, which should be placed as near its antecedent as possible, to prevent ambiguity in the sense, as "The speakers insulted their opponents who attended the meeting," which should be, "The speakers who attended the meeting insulted their opponents."

RULE VI. If no nominative come between the relative and the verb the relative shall be the nominative to the verb; but if a nominative come between them the relative shall be in the objective case, as "God *who* sees us," "God *whom* we worship."

Note 1. In the latter case the relative is frequently omitted, as "The man (whom) I spoke to."

RULE VII. When two or more singular nominatives are joined by *and* the verb following must be plural, as "John and James *were* here."

Note 1. When two or more singular nominatives are united by such expressions as *together with, as well as,* the verb must be singular, as "John as well as James *was* here."

Note 2. A collective noun is followed by a singular or plural verb according as unity or plurality of idea is implied, as "The army *is* large," "The public *are* informed."

RULE VIII. When nominatives of different persons are connected by *or* or *nor* the verb must agree with the one next to it, as "Either James or I *am* wrong."

Note 1. When nominatives of the *same* person are connected by *or* or *nor* the verb must be singular, as "Neither Robert nor his brother *is* industrious."

Note 2. When one nominative is plural the verb must agree with it, the plural nominative being placed next to the verb, as "Neither he nor they are to be believed."

RULE IX. When a noun or pronoun and a participle come together, their case depending on no other word in the sentence, they are said to be in the *nominative absolute,* as "*He being leader* we shall be safe," "*The lessons being finished* we may play."

GOVERNMENT.

RULE X. One noun governs another signifying a different thing in the possessive case, as "God's law."

Note 1. When two nouns in the possessive are in apposition the sign of the possessive is put after the latter only, as "Johnson the barber's."

Note 2. When several nouns in the possessive come together the sign of the possessive is put after the last only, as "James, Harry, and William's pens;" but when they are separated by certain words, the sign is added to each, as "Harry's as well as William's pens."

Note 3. The objective case with *of* often takes the place of the possessive, as "My brother's friend," "The friend of my brother."

RULE XI. Transitive verbs and their participles govern the objective case, as "I saw *her,*" "Hearing *him* was enough."

Note 1. Some sentences have an indirect object, which is sometimes formed by a noun in apposition, and sometimes governed by a preposition, as "He appointed Cæsar *dictator,*" "They accused him *of theft.*"

Note 2. Some verbs in the passive voice are followed by an objective, "He was taught grammar."

Note 3. When the relative is preceded by *than* it is put in the objective case, as "Your brother than *whom* I never met a more intelligent man."

RULE XII. Double comparisons should never be used, as "He is more wiser than his brother," which should be, "He is wiser than his brother."

Note 1. This usage, however, was considered grammatical in the time of Shakspeare, as " That was the *most unkindest* cut of all."

Note 2. The comparative degree should be used when comparison is instituted between two, or between one and a number taken collectively, as " He is richer than I," " He is richer than the whole company."

Note 3. The superlative should be used when comparison is made between one and any number, as " He is the richest of the company."

RULE XIII. One verb governs another in the infinitive mood as " I desire *to learn."*

Note 1. Bid, *need, dare, make, see, feel, observe,* and some others, are followed by the infinitive without *to,* as " He bade me read," " You need not *tell."*

RULE XIV. Adverbs come after verbs, before adjectives, and between the auxiliary and the principal as " She speaks *well,"* " He is *remarkably* diligent," " The pupils are *well* taught."

Note 1. Two negatives in the same sentence destroy each other and are equivalent to an affirmative, as " I did not say nothing," that is, " I did say something."

Note 2. Sometimes two negatives are used as an affirmative, as " He was not unmindful of his duty."

Note 3. The Anglo-Saxons used three negatives, and in modern French *ne-pas* is equivalent to *not ; ne-jamais* to *never ;* and *ne-que* to *only.*

RULE XV. Prepositions govern nouns and pronouns in the objective case, as " Come to *me,"* " Give it to *her."*

Note 1. The preposition is generally put before the word it governs, as " I spoke to the servant."

Note 2. The chief exceptions are the relative pronoun, interrogative sentences, and poetry, as " The man *whom* I relied on," " *Him* did you give it to ? "

Note 3. Certain words require particular prepositions after them, as *liable to, worthy of, abide by, averse from,* &c.

RULE XVI. Conjunctions connect like cases and moods, as " I love *him* and *her,"* " They neither *see* nor *hear."*

Note 1. Co-ordinate conjunctions connect sentences which are independent, as " John came yesterday *and* went away to-day."

Note 2. Subordinate conjunctions connect sentences one of which is dependent on, or subordinate to, the other, as " I will go *if* you will accompany me."

RULE XVII. Interjections govern pronouns of the first person in the nominative, and pronouns of the second person in the objective case, as " Ah, me ! " " Oh, thou unfortunate one ! "

ANALYSIS OF SENTENCES.

By analysis of sentences is meant, resolving a sentence into its different elements or constituent parts.

A sentence is a complete thought expressed in language.

Sentences are either *simple, complex,* or *compound.*

THE SIMPLE SENTENCE.

The simple sentence consists of one subject or nominative and one finite verb, as "Birds sing."

Note.—Every sentence must consist of two parts. In speaking or writing there must be (1) something to discourse about, which is the subject; and (2) something to assert concerning this subject, which is called the *predicate,* as—

Subject.	Predicate.
Birds	sing.

These may be indefinitely enlarged or extended, as—

Subject.	Predicate.
Some birds	sing sweetly.

The Subject.

The *subject* may be either *simple* or *enlarged.*
The simple subject may consist of

1.	*A noun*	as Birds sing.
2.	*Pronoun*	He reads.
3.	*Adjective*	The wise are happy.
4.	*Infinitive*	To forgive is divine.
5.	*Participle*	Walking is beneficial.
6.	*Phrase*	"A Midsummer Night's Dream" is a fine drama.

The enlarged subject may be formed by

1.	*An adjective*	Some birds sing.
2.	*Possessive*	Robert's book is lost.
3.	*Noun in apposition*	Cicero the orator was killed.
4.	*Prepositional phrase*	The time of winter is come.
5.	*Participal*	Cæsar, having conquered, returned to Gaul.
6.	*Infinitival*	The desire to live is natural.

E

The Predicate.

The *predicate* may be either *simple* or *extended*.

The **simple** predicate is either a verb, or the verb *to be* followed by some word or phrase necessary to complete the sense.

1. *Intransitive verb*	Fishes swim.
2. *Transitive verb*	John tears his book.
3. *" To be" and a noun*	He is a genius.
4. *" To be" and an adjective*	They are foolish.
5. *" To be" and a phrase*	We are to be commended.

The Object.

When the predicate is a transitive verb an *object* is required to complete the sense, as—

The master taught the pupil.

Note.—Sometimes the sentence is regarded as being composed of three parts, the *subject, predicate,* and *object.* The object is now generally treated as the completion of the predicate.

The **object** may be enlarged in the same manner as the subject.

1. *An object in apposition*	They consider him a poet.
2. *An indirect object*	They gave money to the poor.
3. *Adjective*	The father loves his dear children.
4. *Prepositional phrase*	We honour the man of understanding.
5. *Infinitival phrase*	The master teaches the pupils to be honest.

The **predicate** is also enlarged by various words and phrases.

1. *An Adverb*	She sang well.
2. *An adverbial phrase*	He spoke indeed most eloquently.
3. *A prepositional*	He marched with a large army.
4. *A participal*	The sun rises gladdening the earth.
5. *An infinitival*	He desires to do good.
6. *The nominative absolute*	He will set out weather permitting.

The various enlargements of the subject and extensions the predicate are also called *adjuncts.*

The adjuncts of the predicate are classed into those of *time, place, manner, cause, instrument,* &c.

ANALYSIS OF SIMPLE SENTENCES.

Example 1.

Now cold winter wraps his icy mantle all around.

Subject.	Predicate.
Cold winter	now wraps his icy mantle all around.

Winter	simple subject.
Cold	enlargement of subject.
Wraps	simple predicate.
Mantle	object, completion of predicate.
His icy	adjective, enlargement of object.
All around	adverb, enlargement of predicate.

Example 2.

The victorious Cæsar having subdued Britain, resolved to secure his conquest by exacting hostages?

Subject.	Predicate.
The victorious Cæsar, having subdued Britain,	resolved to secure his conquest by exacting hostages.
1. Cæsar	simple subject.
2. The victorious	adjective, enlargement of subject.
3. Having subdued Britain	participal phrase, enlargement of subject.
1. Resolved	simple predicate.
2. To secure his conquest	infinitival phrase, completion of predicate.
3. By exacting hostages	prepositional phrase, extention of predicate.

TABULAR FORM OF ANALYSIS.

Subject with enlargement if any.	Predicate.	Object with enlargement if any.	Extensions of predicate.
The victorious Cæsar having subdued Britain,	resolved	to secure his conquest	by exacting hostages.

Exercise 25.

Analyse the following simple sentences.

1. John loves Robert. 2. John's father sold his horse. 3. A good man is always happy. 4. The wicked child broke the glass with a stone. 5. The studious man labours constantly to improve his mind by study. 6. The kingdom of Israel was divided into two parts in the reign of Soloman's successor. 7. The thief, having secured his prey, decamped with the booty, in hot haste. 8. The chairman, having first addressed the meeting, introduced the lecturer to the audience with a few remarks. 9. Now is the winter of our discontent made glorious summer by the sun of York.

THE COMPLEX SENTENCE.

The complex sentence is composed of two or more simple sentences some of which are dependent on another.

That part containing the main assertion is called the *principal* sentence, and those dependent on it are called *subordinate.*

Subordinate sentences take the place of a *noun,* an *adjective,* or an *adverb.* They are therefore of three kinds, the *noun sentence,* the *adjective sentence,* and the *adverb sentence.*

The Noun sentence is so called because it is equal in value to a noun. It may be either the subject or object of a verb, and must begin either with the conjunction *that,* an interrogative pronoun, or an adverb, as—

1. *That he will yield* is certain.
2. *What course I may take* is doubtful.
3. I perceive *how it happened.*

The connective *that* may be omitted when the sentence is a direct quotation, as

"He replied (that) 'All men are mortal.'"

The Adjective sentence is so called because it is equal in value to an adjective. It may qualify either the subject or object, and must begin either with a relative pronoun, or such substitutes, as *whence, wherein, when, why,* &c.

1. The man *who provides for the future* is wise.
2. They built the house *which had fallen.*
3. The house *wherein you stand* is old.

The Adverb sentence is so called because it is equal in value to an adverb. Adverb sentences may be classified in the same way as ordinary adverbial adjuncts, as those of *time, place, manner, cause,* &c.

1. *Time.* He looked on *while his house was burning.*
2. *Place.* Put that back *where you found it.*
3. *Manner.* I will do *as you desire me.*
4. *Cause.* I love him *because he is obedient.*
5. *Effect.* As a man sows *so will he reap.*
6. *Condition.* You ought not to live *unless you work.*

When subordinate sentences are of the same rank or value, they are said to be *co-subordinate,* as—

There was a time *when you were honest,* and *paid your debts.*

Here the last two are independent of each other, and both dependent on the first. They are therefore *co-subordinate.*

ANALYSIS OF COMPLEX SENTENCES.

"The very intelligence, which, in individual cases, is necessary to contentment, forbids in the case of nations, every feeling of satisfaction."

1. The very intelligence	subject to principal pred. 4.
2. which is necessary to	subord. adj. sentence qualifying 1.
contentment	prepos. phrase extension of 2.
3. in individual cases	
4. forbids	principal predicate
5. in the case of nations	prepos. phrase, extension of 4.
6. every feeling of satisfaction.	object, completion of 4.

TABULAR ANALYSIS.

Sentence given.	Kind.	Subject (with enlargement if any).	Predicate.	Object, &c.	Extension of predicate.
a. The very intelligence forbids in the case of nations every feeling of satisfaction.	principal to *b.*	The very intelligence	forbids	every feeling of satisfaction	in the case of nations
b. which, in individual cases is necessary to contentment	subord. to *a.*	which	is necessary	to contentment.	in individual cases.

Exercise 26.

Analyse the following complex sentences.

1. I believe that you are honest. 2. I honour him who speaks the truth. 3. I know not what he will do. 4. This is the place where he was born. 5. The place whereon thou standest is holy ground. 6. He looked on calmly while others stood aghast. 7. I will endeavour to act as you desire. 8. He met with much success in life because he studied to deserve it. 9. I cannot undertake such a duty unless you will assist me in its performance. 10. He was generally esteemed in the town because he laboured for the good of others and considered the wants of the poor.

THE COMPOUND SENTENCE.

A compound sentence consists of two or more principal sentences co-ordinate with each other, as—

Virtue adorns man, but vice degrades him.

Co-ordinate sentences are of four kinds, according to the relation in which they stand to each other—*copulative, alternative, adversative,* and *causative.*

1. **Copulative,** where two or more co-ordinate are joined in structure and meaning, as—

Robert plays, and James sings.

Copulative conjunctions :—*and, also, both, indeed, further, more, likewise, moreover, neither, nor, as well as,* &c.

2. **Alternative** (or disjunctive), where joined in structure, but disconnected in meaning, as—

They will either cure or kill him.

Alternative conjunctions :—*either, or, else, otherwise.*

3. **Adversative,** where joined in structure, but opposed or contrasted in meaning, as—

The world passeth away, but the word of God endureth for ever.

Adversative conjunctions :—*but, yet, however, still, nevertheless, notwithstanding.*

4. **Causative** (or illative), where joined in structure,

the latter expressing an effect or consequence of the former, as—

He formerly behaved dishonestly, hence the people distrusted him.

Causative conjunctions :—*accordingly, because, for, consequently, hence, therefore, whence, wherefore.*

Co-ordinate sentences are frequently contrasted by the omission of the subject, predicate, or object, to avoid the too frequent repetition of the same word or words, when they are called *elliptical*, as—

1. John reads (well), and (John) writes well.
2. Robert (struck the dog), George (struck the dog), and Peter struck the dog.

In analysing elliptical sentences, the omitted parts should be first supplied thus—

ANALYSIS OF COMPOUND SENTENCES.

Example 1.

The pupils always behaved well, and gave the master satisfaction.

A. The pupils always, &c.	Principal sentence co-ordi- with B.
The pupils	subject.
behaved	predicate.
well	extension of pred. (manner.)
always	extension of pred. (time.)
B. And the pupils gave, &c.	Principal sentence in cop. co-ordin. with A.
The pupils	subject.
gave	predicate
the master	indir. object, compl. of predicate.
satisfaction	object, completion of predicate.

Example 2.

The behaviour of the pupil was excellent, therefore the master was pleased.

A. The behaviour of the pupil, &c.	Principal sentence co-ord. inate with *B.*
the behaviour	subject.
of the pupil	prepos. enlargement of subject.
was	predicate.
excellent.	completion of predicate.
B. Therefore the master, &c.	Principal sentence in *caus.* co-ord. with *A.*
The master	subject.
was	predicate.
pleased	completion of predicate.

Example 3.

"I wish, after all I have said about wit and humour, I could satisfy myself of the good effects upon the character and disposition; but I am convinced the probable tendency of both is to corrupt the understanding and the heart."

1. I wish,	Principal sentence.
2. After all I have said about wit and humour,	adverb-sentence subord. to 1.
3. (that) I could satisfy myself of the good effects upon the character and disposition,	noun-sentence, completion of 1.
4. but I am convinced	principal sentence in *adv.* co-ord. with 1.
5. (that) the probable tendency of both is	noun-sentence subord. to, and completion of, 4.
6. to corrupt the understanding and the heart.	infinit. object to 5, and completion of 4.

This may be much elaborated according to examples already given.

TABULAR ANALYSIS.

Sentence.	Kind.	Subject (with enlargement if any).	Predicate.	Object (with enlargement).	Extensions.
a. I wish,	princip. s. co-ordinate with *d.*	I	wish		after all
b. after all I have said about wit and humour,	adverb-s. subord. to *a.*	I	have said	*(indirect)* about wit and humour	
c. I could satisfy myself of the good effects upon the character and disposition;	noun-s. sub-ord. to, and comp. of, *a.*	I	could satisfy	myself *(indirect)* of the good effects upon the character and disposition	
d. but I am convinced,	princip. s. in *adv.* co-ord. with *a.*	I	am convinced		
e. the probable tendency of both is to corrupt the understanding and the heart.	noun-s. sub-ord. to, and comp. of, *d.*	the probable tendency	is	to corrupt the understanding and the heart.	

Exercise 27.

Analyse the following compound sentences.

1. John is foolish, and often commits mistakes. 2. Run to the station, or you will be too late. 3. Either you or I am mistaken. 4. James hurt his sister, but she willingly forgave him. 5. Though he fall, yet he shall not be utterly destroyed. 6. He was unable to set sail, for the wind was contrary. 7. He has been detected in the theft, hence his sudden departure has surprised no one. 8. Horses, dogs, and sheep are swift animals, and are very useful to man.

10. Having often received an invitation from my friend Sir Roger de Coverly to pass away a month with him in the country, I last week accompanied him thither, and am settled with him for some time at his country house, where I intend to form several of my ensuing speculations.

11. From Jesse's root behold a branch arise,
Whose sacred flower with fragrance fills the skies :
The Ethereal Spirit o'er its leaves shall move,
And on its top descend the mystic dove.

COMPOSITION.

Elegance in composition is only to be attained by strict attention to punctuation, and the choice of words ; and by the study of the best writers.

PUNCTUATION.

The various points in use are—

The *comma* (,), used for a short pause, as "In that special case, he acted with discretion."

The *semicolon* (;), when a larger pause is necessary and the sentences are co-ordinate, as "The course is clear ; the race glorious to run."

The *colon* (:), where a still longer pause is necessary to make the sense apparent, as "'Tis past : the iron north has spent his rage."

The *period* (.), used at the close of a sentence.

The *point of interrogation* (?), used at the end of a question.

The *point of exclamation* (!), used after interjections and ejaculatory sentences, as "Sweet sounds! that oft have soothed to rest."

The *parenthesis* ( ), includes an expression not directly dependent on any other, and the omission of which does not disturb the meaning of the rest, as "And who commanded (and the silence came), 'Here let the billows stiffen, and have rest.'"

The *dash* (—), indicates a pause without breaking the connection or the relation of the preceding and following parts of the sentence, as " You saw the greatest warrior of the age—conqueror of Italy—humbler of Germany."

The *quotation* (" "), indicates that the sentence has been spoken or written before.

The *diæresis* (··), shows that two vowels coming together are each sounded, as " äerial."

The *accents* are, the acute ('), the grave (`), the circumflex (^), the long (¯), the short (˘),

Other marks used in composition are the asterisk(*), the obelisk or dagger (†), the section (§), the parallel (‖), the paragraph (¶), the index or hand (☞), the asterismus (*⁎*), the cedilla (ҫ), and the caret (ʌ).

CAPITAL LETTERS.

Capital letters are used in the following positions.—
1. The first word of every sentence.
2. The first word of every line of poetry.
3. The first word of a direct quotation.
4. Names of the supreme being.
5. Proper nouns, and adjectives derived from them.
6. Names of the days, months, and terms.
7. Any very important or particular word.
8. The chief words in titles of books, &c.
9. The names of objects personified.
10. The pronoun I and interjections O! and Oh!

Exercise 28.

Point the following, and rectify the mistakes in letters.

most persons say that the only purpose of music is to amuse But this is a profane an unholy Language to look on Music as mere amusement Cannot be justified music which has no other Aim must be considered neither of Value nor worthy of reverence. Thus spake plato and his opinion is shared by those who are striving to spread music Among the people in the present Day.

    rome for Empire far renowned
    tramples on a thousand States
    soon her Pride shall kiss the ground
    hark the gaul is at her Gates.

TAUTOLOGY.

Tautology means a repetition of the same idea in different words, or a useless repetition of the same word, as—

He gained the *universal* esteem of *all* men.
They cut down *entirely* the *whole* forest.

PLEONASM.

Pleonasm is a redundancy of words in speaking or writing, or the use of more words than are actually necessary to express one's meaning, as—

I saw it *with my own eyes*.
Where *in the world* is he?

ELLIPSIS.

Ellipsis means the leaving out of certain words not absolutely necessary to the right understanding of the sentence, as—

Where is the book (which) you bought?
He speaks more correctly than you (speak).

FIGURES OF SPEECH.

When we say what we mean in *plain language*, we are said to speak *literally*. Sometimes, however, we can speak and write with more emphasis by the presentation of one truth for the sake of enforcing another, and this is called *figurative* speech.

The various figures of speech are *simile, metaphor, allegory, metonymy, personification, synechdoche, hyperbole, antithesis, irony, climax,* and *apostrophe.*

A simile is a figure by which two things are compared, which, though essentially different, have points of resemblance, as—

The *path* of the just is as the *shining light.*

A metaphor is a figure expressing resemblance to another in some particular character, as—

Newton, the great *luminary* of science.

An allegory is a figurative sentence or discourse, in which one truth is taught by presenting another, as—

Give ear, O *Shepherd* of Israel! thou that leadest Joseph like *a flock.*

The eightieth Psalm and the Pilgrim's Progress are allegories.

Metonymy is that figure by which the meaning of

F

one word is conveyed by another, each having a certain dependence on, or relation to, the other, as—

> The *cup* that cheers but not inebriates.
> It is the production of an elegant *pen.*

Synechdoche is a figure in which the whole is put for a part, or a part for the whole, as—

> He has gained the esteem of the *world.*
> He employs many *hands.*

Personification is that figure by which we ascribe to inanimate objects the attributes of living beings, as—

> The mountains *shout for joy.*

Hyperbole is a figure by which things are represented as greater or less, better or worse, than they really are, as—

> He ran as quick as *lightning.*
> They were as ignorant as the *brutes.*

Antithesis is a mode of expression by which the meaning is rendered more impressive by comparison or contrast, as—

> On one side stands *modesty,* on the other *impudence;* on one *fidelity,* on the other *deceit;* here *piety,* there *sacrilege.*

Irony is the expression of an opposite sense to that which we wish to convey, and is meant to express derision or contempt, as—

> Napoleon was a truly humble-minded man.
> Go, now, and study tuneful verse at Rome.

Horace uses this expression after graphically describing the noise and tumult of the city.

Climax is that mode of expression by which the writer intensifies his meaning by gradually ascending from the less to the more significant element in the expression, as—

> What a piece of work is man! how noble in reason! how infinite in faculties! in form and motion how expressive and admirable! in action how like an angel! in apprehension how like a god!

Apostrophe is a mode of expression by which we directly address some object living or dead, as—

> O *Thou* that hearest prayer!
> Why art thou cast down, O! *my soul?*
> *Vital spark* of heavenly flame!
> Quit, oh, quit this mortal frame!

Exercise 29.

Distinguish the figures of speech, and point out instances of tautology, pleonasm, and ellipsis :—

1. Have you read Cicero? 2. He bought fifty head of cattle. 3. Charles II. was a truly virtuous prince. 4. He runs like a deer. 5. O, Absalom! my son, my son! 6. The trees rejoice with the return of spring. 7. I never like to play second fiddle. 8. The eloquence of Demosthenes was like an impetuous torrent. 9. Righteousness exalteth a nation, but sin is a reproach to any people. 10. We are called upon as members of this house, as men, as Christians, to protest against this horrible barbarity. 11. She was fair as a flower in June. 12. Thy word is a light unto my feet, and a lamp unto my path. 13. Let us retire backwards. 14. The whole country was indignant. 15. He did it with his own hands. 16. Many men, many minds. 17. O, Jerusalem! Jerusalem! Thou that killest the prophets and stonest them that are sent unto thee! 18. You do nothing, you attempt nothing, you think nothing, but what I not only hear, but also see, and plainly perceive.

CHAPTER IV.
PROSODY.

Prosody is that part of grammar which treats of the different modes of speaking and reading, and of the different kinds of verse.

The art of correct speaking and reading consists in the proper use of *pause, accent, emphasis,* and *intonation,* which regulate the occurrence of *metre.*

Metre has been defined as "The recurrence within certain intervals of syllables similarly affected."

Pause is a short cessation of the voice to give clearness or impressiveness to the utterances of the speaker, as—

Your employment on the last night—your occupations on the preceding night—the place where you met—the persons who met—and the plot fabricated at the meeting :— of these things, I ask not who knows; I ask, who, among you all is ignorant?—*Cicero against Catiline.*

Accent is a particular stress laid on a part of a word, as, *excél, éxcellent.*

Emphasis is a stress laid on part of a sentence, which, when used with propriety, adds beauty and impressiveness to the significance of language. It is not confined to any particular word, but may vary according to the intended meaning. It may be illustrated in the following sentence :—

Are you going to town to-day? Are *you* going to town to-day? Are you *going* to town to-day? Are you going to *town* to-day? Are you going to town *to-day?* A different reply may be given to each.

Intonation is that modulation of the voice, suited to the sentiments of the speaker, known as the rising and falling inflections, as—

I *cannot*, my lords, I WILL NOT, *join* in congratulations on misfortune and disgrace.

Note.—In speaking the voice rises gradually, or *slides* from one tone to another; while in singing it *leaps* from note to note. The distinction may be illustrated by the difference between a sliding scale and a stair.

VERSE.

Verse is the arrangement of syllables in regular order or succession, according to certain laws.

Note.—The distinction between the accent in poetry and prose is, that while in the former it is regular and fixed, in the latter it is irregular, uncertain, and, to a considerable extent, regulated by the speaker.

Verse is of two kinds, *rhyme* and *blank verse.*

In **Rhyme** the final syllables correspond in sound.

In **Blank Verse** the final syllables do not correspond in sound.

Every line of poetry consists of a certain number of *feet.*

A **foot** in poetry means the periodic return of a series of syllables similarly accented.

The following names, borrowed from the Greek and Latin, have been applied to English poetry :—

A Trochee,	– ˘	A Dactyl,	– ˘ ˘
An Iambus,	˘ –	An Amphibrach,	˘ – ˘
A Spondee,	– –	An Anapaest,	˘ ˘ –
A Pyrrhic,	˘ ˘	A Tribrach,	˘ ˘ ˘

Trochaic verse consists of an accented and an unaccented syllable, and may be formed of various numbers of feet, as—

Jésus, lóver óf my sóul,
Lét me tó Thy bósom flý.

Iambic verse consists of an unaccented and an accented syllable, as—

> Of mán's first disobédience, ánd the fráit
> Of thát forbídden trée, whose mórtal táste
> Brought déath intó this wórld and áll our wóe.

Dactylic consists of one accented and two unaccented syllables, as—

> Knów ye the lánd where the cýpress and mýrtle
> Are émblems of déeds that are dóne in their clíme?

Anapaestic consists of two unaccented and one accented syllable, as—

> Who are théy that now bíd us be sláves?
> They are fóes to the góod and the frée.

Sometimes the line pauses through the omission of one or more syllables of the foot.

The line indicating this pause is called the *cæsura*, thus—

> Begoné unbelíef | my Sáviour is néar,
> And fór my relíef | will súrely appeár.

This ommission frequently occurs at the end of the line—

> Oné more unfórtunate
> Wéary of bréath, |
> Ráshly impórtunate,
> Góne to her déath! |

The above specimens sufficiently illustrate the character of English metres. The others are of rare occurrence, and unsuited to the genius of the English language.

These may comprise various numbers of feet in each line, at the will of the author.

When a line contains one foot it is called *monometer*; when it contains two it is called *dimeter*; when three, *trimeter*; when four, *tetrameter*; when five, *pentameter*; when six, *hexameter*; when seven, *heptameter*; when eight, *octometer*.

These last are of rare occurrence, and generally written as two lines. The "common metre" and "long metre," so much used in hymnody, form *heptameter* and *octometer* when written two lines in one.

The common metre is the same as that so much used by ancient ballad writers, only in a different form.

F 2

The following hymn may be written as follows:

C. M.

There is a land of pure delight,
Where saints immortal reign;
Infinite day excludes the night,
And pleasures banish pain.

Ballad Metre.

There is a land of pure delight where saints immortal reign;
Infinite day excludes the night, and pleasures banish pain.

The ballad similarly may be changed from its original metre into the *C. M.* form.

POETICAL LICENCE.

Poetical Licence is that departure from the rules of grammar rendered necessary by the difficulty of arranging the words in regular measure, according to the number of syllables in a line. The following are different kinds of it:—

Drop upon Fox's grave the tear,
'*Twill* trickle to his rival's bier.

And sends the winter's icy power
T' invigorate *th'* exhausted ground.

They fall *successive* and *successive* rise.

Remote, unfriended, melancholly, slow,
Or by the lazy Scheldt or wandering Po.

CHAPTER V.

THE ENGLISH LANGUAGE.

ITS HISTORY AND CONSTITUENT ELEMENTS.

Any one acquainted with the history of our country will have a pretty accurate idea of the constituent elements of the English Language. He knows, for instance, that the original inhabitants of Britain were Celtic, and will therefore expect to find certain Celtic elements in the language. The Romans governed Britain for about four hundred years, and we may therefore infer that they left their mark on the language of the country. It was not at this time, however, that the chief Latin additions were made to English. What vestiges of Roman rule remain, in this respect, are chiefly found in the names of towns, such as Chester, Lancaster, Doncaster, Lincoln, Pontefract, street, &c. He knows, too, that the English are chiefly descended from the Anglo-Saxons, and naturally infers that Anglo-Saxon must form the groundwork of our language as it does of our race. Next came the Danish rule, and after that the Norman.

When one race conquers another, it endeavours to impose its language on the conquered, as one means of keeping it in subjection, and of destroying the remembrance of its former freedom and independence. Norman French, thus became in England the language of the court, of parliament, and diplomacy. Anglo-Saxon, however, still continued the language of the people, and as the Saxons were by far the most numerous, their language remains the main element in our tongue.

Language has been called "fossil poetry," and appropriately so, for as an acquaintance with fossils reveals to us much of the past history of our globe with respect to its animal and vegetable life, so the study of language in its different stages of growth and development, reveals to us much of the social life of the people, their occupations, customs, manners, virtues, and vices. There is something in the very mode of address which reveals something of the life of the people. For instance, when an Egyptian asks his neighbour "How do you perspire?" we conclude that free perspiration is an essential element in healthy life of the people; and when one Chinese asks another "How is your digestion?" we naturally infer that the wants of the appetite are not overlooked by the celestials. An Italian expression is *umiliare una supplica*, "to humiliate a petition," that is, "to present a memorial." Italy has been called the battle-field of Europe. It has been long oppressed by the "hand of the stranger," till its political humiliation has entered into the social life of the people, and become impressed on their language.

The history of the English language has been divided into five periods.

The *Anglo-Saxon*,—1050, the chief characteristics of which are variety of gender, number, case, and inflections generally, as compared with modern English, some of which have been supplanted by prepositions. It had six declensions, three numbers, a dual form being used in pronouns, and five cases. The sign of the genitive es has been modified into our possessive sign 's. The plural of nouns ended in en, as house, housen, a form still used sometimes by un-educated persons.

The *Semi-Saxon*, 1050-1250.—In this period the Anglo-Saxon becomes mixed with Norman French; inflection begins to decline; declensions are less distinct; the ablative case disappears; and the infinitive of the verb ends in e instead of en, as nemmen, nemine, "to name."

The *Old English*, 1250-1350.—The article "*the*" is now unchanged for gender, but has different case-endings. Gender, which formerly followed the termination of the word, is regulated by sex, as in modern English. The cases in nouns and adjectives, except the accusative, are expressed by prepositions.

The *Middle English*, 1350-1550.—"*The*" is now used for all cases and genders; declensions are reduced to one; the genitive es after changing into is becomes our possessive 's, the participle endings "ende," "ande" and the verbal noun ending "ung," become merged into "ing," which is used both as a present participle and verbal noun, as now.

During the middle Ages, learning and literature were chiefly cultivated by the clergy, and as their studies led them to the perusal of Latin writings, so many of the most valuable productions of this period were written in Latin. During the Middle English period, Italian and French literature flourished, and were admired and studied by English authors. Chaucer, who was a great admirer of French literature, introduced many French words into his writings, and it is during this period that the chief French additions were made to the English language.

At the revival of learning in the sixteenth century, the classical writers of antiquity became models of imitation for British authors, and from this time to that of Milton, the main Latin and Greek additions were introduced, and as science and philosophy were first cultivated by the Greeks, their language has ever been the chief source from which scientific terms have been drawn.

The *Modern English*, 1550.—The English language which, like other modern language, is constantly receiving accessions from all quarters, became now fixed pretty much as we find it.* Constant intercourse with other nations, new manu- factures, fresh discoveries, and inventions in science and art, change of fashion, &c., are continually introducing new terms, to which no limit can be assigned.

When we remember that the two great sources of our language, the Saxon and Latin, are branches of the same Indo-Germanic family, we need not wonder that consider- able difference of opinion exists as to the exact proportion which these bear in English. The general opinion, however, is, that "Modern English dictionaries contain about 38,000 words, exclusive of preterites and participles; of this number 23,000 have been found on examination to be from the Saxon; i.e., about 25-40ths (or 5-8ths) of the whole. And this fraction represents, with approximate accuracy, the pro- portion of Saxon words in common use."† About 2-8ths are derived from the Latin, and the remaining 1-8th from other sources. As words in common use, such as names of natural objects, terms of social intercourse and endear- ment, &c., are chiefly Saxon, our ordinary conversation contains a considerably larger proportion of Saxon words, and as poetry is less affected by modern discoveries than prose, it contains a larger proportion of Saxon words than prose; hence the study of poetry has been recommended as a means of cultivating a Saxon style. The greatest living poet, Tennyson, is also one of the most Saxon of writers.

Words are of two kinds, *roots* and *derivatives*.

A **root** is a word in the simplest or original state, or that cannot be further traced to its original sources, as *son, love, go, come, strong, shake*.

A **primary derivative** is a root slightly altered in form without the addition of prefix or suffix as *drank* from *drink, led* from *lead, hung* from *hang, strength* from *strong, glaze* from *glass*.

A **secondary derivative** is a word formed from the root by the addition of a prefix or suffix, or another word, as *loving, sweetly, strengthen, glazier, manhood, buttercup*.

---

* The word "its" is a prominent exception. It is not in the English Bible of 1611, "his" being used instead. Shakspere is the first to use it. It is also found, though seldom, in Milton.

† Angus's "Handbook of the English Tongue," p. 4.

Note.—Distinction must be made between a root and a stem, the former being the original word, the latter that part to which the inflections are added.

The following are specimens of English words naturalised from foreign sources. Many more might be given.

1. *Celtic.*—Basket, button, kiln, darn, gown, mop.
2. *Danish.*—Derby, Whitby, din, doze, fling, rap.
3. *French.*—Beef, cry, coach, damsel, eclat, mutton.
4. *Italian.*—Bandit, buffet, forte, piano, tassel, gazette.
5. *Spanish.*—Anchovy, armada, barrack, hurricane, cigar, negro.
6. *Portuguese.*—Caste, coco, fetish, marmalade, palaver.
7. *German.*—Howl, huddle, rifle, rudder, waltz.
8. *Dutch.*—Blow, dog, freight, schooner, sloop, yacht.
9. *Hebrew.*—Amen, cabala, cherub, ephod, Satan, seraph.
10. *Arabic.*—Admiral, alchemy, algebra, chemistry, coffee, zenith.
11. *Persian.*—Azure, caravan, dervish, lilac, scarlet.
12. *Turkish.*—Divan, dragoman, janissaries, scimitar, turban.
13. *Chinese.*—Bohea, Congou, gong, nankeen, pagoda, tea.
14. *Malay.*—Banham, gamboge, sago, shaddock.
15. *Indian.*—Calico, chintz, curry, lac, muslin, toddy.
16. *Polynesian.*—Taboo, tatoo.
17. *West Indian.*—Maize, potatoes, tobacco.
18. *American.*—Hammock, jerked, squaw, wigwam.

Many others might be given, derived from persons, places, occasions, &c., which have given them birth, such as damask, currants, tantalize, meander, herculean, philippics, &c.

PREFIXES AND SUFFIXES.

A **prefix** is a syllable prefixed to a word to alter its meaning.

A **suffix** is a syllable added to the end of a word to alter its meaning.

I. SAXON PREFIXES.

A, *on, or in,*	as ashore		Out, *beyond,*	as outrun
Be, *about,*	„ bespatter		Over, *excess,*	„ overwork
For, *opposition,*	„ forbid		Un, *not,*	„ undo
Fore, *before,*	„ foresee		Under, *beneath,*	„ understate
In, *en, on,*	„ enthrone		Up, *upwards,*	„ upraise
„ *to make,*	„ encircle		With, *against,*	„ withstand
Mis, *error,*	„ mistake			

II. SAXON SUFFIXES.

Forming Nouns.

1. *The Agent or Doer.*

Ar,	as liar
Ard,	„ drunkard
Ary,	„ secretary
Er,	„ leader
Or,	„ sailor
Ster,	„ songster
Yer,	„ lawyer

2. *The Object.*

Ee,	„ trustee

3. *Act, State, Being.*

Age,	„ bondage
Dom,	„ freedom
Hood,	„ manhood
Ness,	„ kindness
Ry,	„ slavery
Ship,	„ hardship
Th,	„ health
Ter,	„ laughter
Try,	„ gallantry

4. *Diminutives.*

El,	„ satchel
Et,	„ pocket
Kin,	„ lambkin
Le,	„ thimble
Let,	„ streamlet
Ling,	„ darling
Ock,	„ hillock
Ow,	„ shadow

Forming Verbs.

1. *To Make.*

En,	as harden
Er,	„ glimmer
Ish,	„ finish
Le,	„ twinkle

Forming Adjectives.

1. *Denoting Fulness.*

Ed,	„ learned
Ful,	„ truthful
Some,	„ irksome
Y,	„ pithy

2. *Likeness.*

Ish,	„ foolish
Like,	„ warlike
Ly,	„ manly

3. *Belonging to.*

En,	„ wooden
Ern,	„ northern

4. *Without.*

Less,	„ hopeless

Forming Adverbs.

Denoting Manner, Direction.

Ly,	„ boldly
Ward,	„ hitherward

III. LATIN PREFIXES.

A, *ab, abs, from,* as avert		De, *down,* as dethrone
Ad, *to,* „ ashore		Dis, *asunder,* „ discuss
Am, *round,* „ ambition		E, *ex, out of,* „ eject
Ante, *before,* „ antecedent		Extra, *beyond,* „ extravagant
Circum, *about,* „ circumference		In, *im, &c., in, into,* „ infuse
Cis, *on this side,* „ cisalpine		„ „ (before adjectives), *not,*
Con, *together,* „ convene		„ impossible
Contra, *against,* „ contradict		Inter, *between,* „ intercept

LATIN PREFIXES—*continued.*

Intro, *within,*	as introduce	
Juxta, *close to,*	,, juxtaposition	
Ob, &c., *against,*	,, obverse	
Per, *through as,*	,, perforate	
Post, *after,*	,, postscript	
Pre, *before,*	,, precede	
Preter, *beyond,*	,, preternatural	
Pro, *forth,*	,, provoke	
Re, *back or against*	,, recede	

Retro, *back,*	as retrospect
Se, *aside,*	,, secede
Sine, *without,*	,, sinecure
Sub, &c., *under,*	,, subscribe
Subter, *under*	,, subterranean
Super, sur, *over*	,, superfine
Trans, *beyond,*	,, transgress
Ultra, *beyond,*	,, ultramontane

IV. LATIN SUFFIXES.

Nouns.

1, *Agent or Doer.*

Ant,	as assistant
Ary,	,, adversary
Ent,	,, student
Eer,	,, engineer
Ier,	,, cashier

2. *The Object.*

Ary,	,, depositary
Ite,	,, favourite
Ive,	,, captive

3. *Act, Condition.*

Ance,	,, assistance
Ancy,	,, infancy
Ce,	,, justice
Cy,	,, efficiency
Ence,	,, dependence
Ency,	,, dependency
Ment,	,, movement
Mony,	,, patrimony
Or,	,, honor
Sion,	,, profession
Tion,	,, pretention
Tude,	,, gratitude
Ty,	,, safety
Ure,	,, nature
Y,	,, misery

4. *Place, Office.*

Ary,	,, granary
Acy,	,, curacy
Chre,	,, sepulchre
Ory,	,, laboratory

5. *Diminutives.*

Cle,	,, particle
Cule,	,, animalcule

Verbs.

To make.

Ate,	as perpetuate
Fy,	,, glorify
Ite,	,, expedite

Adjectives.

1. *Relation, Nature, Possession.*

Aceous,	as herbaceous
Al,	,, regal
An,	,, sylvan
Ane,	,, profane
Ant,	,, abundant
Ar,	,, peculiar
Ary,	,, auxiliary
Ate,	,, affectionate
Ian,	,, christian
Ic,	,, majestic
Ical,	,, classical
Id,	,, frigid
Ile,	,, fragile
Ine,	,, masculine
Ory,	,, perfunctory

2. *Fulness.*

Lent,	,, opulent
Ose,	,, verbose
Ous,	,, precipitous

3. *Capability.*

Ble,	,, probable
Ive,	,, productive

4. *Increase, Causation.*

Ferous,	,, fructiferous
Fic,	,, terrific
Scent,	,, quiescent

V. GREEK PREFIXES.

A, *not*	as apathy	Ex, *out of*	as exodus
Amphi, *double*	,, amphibious	Hyper, *over*	,, hypercritical
Ana, *through*	,, anatomy	Hypo, *under*	,, hypocrite
Anti, *against*	,, antichrist	Meta, *change*	,, metamorphosis
Apo, *from*	,, apostacy	Para, *beside*	,, parable
Cata, *down*	,, cataract	Peri, *round*	,, perimeter
Dia, *through*	,, diameter	Syn, &c., *with* {	syntax
En, *on or in*	,, energy		sympathy
Epi, *upon*	,, epitaph		

VI. GREEK SUFFIXES.

Nouns.

1. *Agent or Doer.*

An, as politician
Ist, ,, botanist

2. *Action, condition, quality.*

E, ,, epitome
Ism, ,, criticism
Ma, ,, panorama
Sis, ,, phasis
Sy, ,, poesy
Y, ,, eulogy

3. *Doctrine or Science.*

Ic, ,, music

Ics, as hydrostatics
Ism, ,, heroism

4. *Diminutives.*

Isk, ,, asterisk

Verbs.

To make or become.

Ise, as colonise
Ize, ,, baptize

Adjectives.

Relation.

Ic, as philosophic
Ical, ,, botanical

SAXON ROOTS WITH DERIVATIVES.

Ac, *an oak*, acorn	Faran, *to go*, ford
Aethel, *noble*, Ethelred	Fedan, *to feed*, food
Bald, *brave*, Ethelbald	Fian, *to hate*, fiend
Beon, *to be*, been	Fleon, *to flee*, fly
Bidan, *to wait*, abide	Fulian, *to corrupt*, foul
Bindan, *to bind*, bind	Fot, *the foot*, foot
Blawan, *to blow*, blast	Freon, *to love*, friend
Boc, *a book*, book	Gabban, *to skoff*, gabble
Bredan, *to nourish*, bread	Gangan, *to go*, gangway
Burne, *a stream*, Ashburne	Geap, *wide*, gap
Ceapian, *to buy*, cheap	Geard, *enclosure*, yard
Ceorl, *a countryman*, churl	God, *good*, God
Cnafan, *a boy*, knave	Grafan, *to dig*, grave
Cryc, *a staff*, crook	Habban, *to have*, behave
Cunnan, *to know*, ken	Haelan, *to heal*, holy
Cyn, *race*, kin	Ham, *a dwelling*, home
Deman, *to judge*, deem	Hefan, *to lift*, heaven
Dragan, *to draw*, drag	Hund, *a dog*, hound
Dun, *a hill*, Dundee	Ing, *a meadow*, Reading
Dwinan, *to fade*, dwindle	Laedan, *to lead*, ladder
Ea, *water*, Anglesey	Laet, *late*, last
Ead, *possession*, Edwin	Magan, *to be able*, may
Eall, *all*, Alfred	Mengan, *to mix*, mingle

G

SAXON ROOTS WITH DERIVATIVES—*continued.*

Mere, *a lake*, Windermere
Mona, *the moon*, month
Neah, *nigh*, near
Nord, *north*, Norwich
Oga, *dread*, ugly
Ranc, *proud*, rank
Reafian, *to rob*, bereave
Sceadan, *to divide*, shade
Sceapan, *to form*, shape
Snican, *to creep*, snake
Seoc, *sick*, sigh
Sean, *to see*, sight
Sped, *success*, speed
Slagan, *to kill*, slay
Spell, *message*, gospel
Spinnan, *to spin*, spider
Spor, *a heel*, spurn
Stepan, *to raise*, step

Styran, *to steer*, stern
Stoc, *a place*, Woodstock
Tellan, *to tell*, tale
Tid, *time*, Shrovetide
Twa, *two*, twain
Thorpe, *a village*, Bishopsthorpe
Wald, *a wood*, weald
Wanian, *to fail*, wane
Weard, *guard*, warden
Wed, *pledge*, wedlock
Wenden, *to go*, wend
Wesan, *to be*, was
Wic, *dwelling*, Berwick
Witan, *to know*, wit, wise
Win, *war*, Godwin
Writham, *to bind*, writhe
Wyrt, *root*, liverwort

LATIN ROOTS WITH DERIVATIVES.

Acer, *sharp*, acrid
Acidus, *sour*, acid
Aequus, *equal*, equality
Aevum, *an age*, co-eval
Ager, *a field*, agriculture
Ago, *I do*, agent
Alo, *I nourish*, aliment
Altus, *high*, altitude
Amo, *I love*, amity
Angulus, *a corner*, angular
Animus, *the mind*, animate
Annus, *a year*, annual
Aperio, *I open*, aperture
Aqua, *water*, aquatic
Arbor, *a tree*, arbour
Aro, *I plough*, arable
Artus, *a joint*, article
Asper, *rough*, aspirate
Audio, *I hear*, audience
Avis, *a bird*, aviary
Beatus, *blessed*, beatitude
Bibo, *I drink*, imbibe
Brevis, *short*, brevity
Caedo, *I cut*, suicide
Calor, *heat*, caloric
Canis, *a dog*, canine
Capio, *I take*, capture
Caput, *the head*, capital
Caro, *flesh*, carnal
Carus, *dear*, caress
Celer, *swift*, celerity
Centum, *a hundred*, century

Charta, *paper*, charter
Civis, *a citizen*, civil
Claudo, *I shut*, exclude
Coelum, *heaven*, celestial
Colo, *I cultivate*, colony
Cor, *the heart*, concord
Corpus, *the body*, corpse
Credo, *I trust*, credible
Crux, *a cross*, crucify
Culpa, *a fault*, culpable
Curro, *I run*, excursion
Dens, *a tooth*, dentist
Deus, *a god*, deity
Dico, *I say*, dictate
Dies, *a day*, diary
Doceo, *I teach*, docile
Domus, *a house*, domestic
Duco, *I lead*, induce
Duo, *two*, duel
Edo, *I eat*, edible
Emo, *I buy*, redeem
Facilis, *easy*, facilitate
Fallo, *I deceive*, infallible
Felix, *happy*, felicity
Fido, *I trust*, confide
Filius, *a son*, filial
Finis, *an end*, final
Flecto, *I bend*, reflect
Flos, *a flower*, floral
Folium, *a leaf*, foliage
Fortis, *strong*, fortify
Frater, *a brother*, fraternal

LATIN ROOTS WITH DERIVATIVES—*continued*.

Fugio, *I flee*, refuge
Fundo, *I pour out*, refund
Gens, *a nation*, Gentile
Gigno, *I beget*, progeny
Gradior, *I go*, gradual
Gravis, *heavy*, gravity
Habeo, *I have*, inhabit
Homo, *a man*, homicide
Hostis, *an enemy*, hostile
Ignis, *fire*, ignite
Imperium, *power*, imperial
Initium, *a beginning*, initiate
Insula, *an island*, insular
Jaceo, *I lie*, adjacent
Jacio, *I throw*, interjection
Judex, *a judge*, judicial
Jungo, *I join*, juncture
Juro, *I swear*, conjure
Jus, *a law*, justice
Latus, *a side*, lateral
Lex, *a law*, legal
Liber, *a book*, library.
Linquo, *I leave*, relinquish
Litera, *a letter*, literal
Locus, *a place*, locality
Loquor, *I speak*, elocution
Ludo, *I play*, illusion
Lumen, *a light*, illuminate
Luna, *the moon*, lunar
Lux, *light*, lucid
Magnus, *great*, magnify
Mando, *I bid*, command
Maneo, *I stay*, permanent
Manus, *a hand*, manual
Mare, *the sea*, marine
Mars, *the god of war*, martial
Mater, *a mother*, maternal
Medius, *the middle*, mediator
Mens, *the mind*, mental
Migro, *I remove*, migratory
Miles, *a soldier*, military
Miror, *I gaze*, mirror
Mitis, *mild*, mitigate
Mitto, *I send*, remit
Moneo, *I warn*, admonish
Monstro, *I show*, demonstrate
Mors, *death*, mortal
Moveo, *I move*, remove
Multus, *many*, multiply
Munus, *a gift*, remunerate
Muto, *I change*, mutable
Navis, *a ship*, naval
Nego, *I deny*, negative

Noceo, *I hurt*, innocent
Neuter, *neither*, neutral
Nomen, *a name*, nominate
Nox, *the night*, nocturnal
Numerus, *a number*, numerate
Nutrio, *I nourish*, nutriment
Oculus, *the eye*, ocular
Opto, *I wish*, adopt
Opus, *a work*, operate
Orbis, *a circle*, orbit
Orior, *I rise*, oriental
Ovum, *an egg*, oval
Pando, *I spread*, expand
Pasco, *I feed*, pastor
Pater, *a father*, paternal
Pauper, *poor*, pauperism
Pax, *peace*, pacify
Pecunia, *money*, pecuniary
Pene, *almost*, peninsula
Pes, *a foot*, pedestal
Pingo, *I paint*, picts
Plebs, *the common people*, plebian
Poena, *punishment*, penal
Pono, *I place*, deposit
Porto, *I carry*, export
Potens, *powerful*, potentate
Primus, *first*, primary
Prosodia, *prosody*
Puer, *a boy*, puerile
Puto, *I think*, reputable
Quaero, *I ask*, question
Radius, *a ray*, radiate
Radix, *a root*, radical
Ramus, *a branch*, ramify
Rapio, *I seize*, rapacious
Rectus, *straight*, rectilineal
Rego, *I rule*, rector
Rideo, *I laugh*, deride
Rodo, *I gnaw*, corrode
Rota, *a wheel*, rotate
Rumen, *the throat*, ruminate
Rus, *the country*, rural
Sal, *salt*, saline
Sanctus, *holy*, sanctify
Scando, *I climb*, ascend
Scio, *I know*, science
Scribo, *I write*, scriptures
Seco, *I cut*, dissect
Secundus, *second*, secondary
Semi, *half*, semicircle
Sequor, *I follow*, sequence
Sidus, *a star*, sidereal

LATIN ROOTS WITH DERIVATIVES—*continued.*

Silva, *a wood,* silvan
Socius, *a companion,* social
Sol, *the sun,* solar
Solvo, *I pay,* solvent
Sors, *a lot,* assort
Species, *a form,* specific
Spiro, *I breathe,* conspire
Spondeo, *I promise,* respond
Stella, *a star,* constellation
Sterilis, *barren,* sterility
Stillo, *I drop,* distil
Sto, *I stand,* stature
Struo, *I build,* structure
Suavis, *sweet,* suavity
Sumo, *I take,* assume
Tango, *I touch,* tangent
Tego, *I cover,* protect
Tempus, *time,* temporal
Terminus, *a boundary,* terminate
Terra, *the earth,* terrestrial
Tertius, *third,* tertiary
Testis, *a witness,* testify
Tollo, *I lift up,* extol
Traho, *I draw,* extract
Trudo, *I thrust,* intrude
Tumeo, *I swell,* tumour
Turpis, *base,* turpitude
Umbra, *a shadow,* umbrella
Unda, *a wave,* undulate
Urbs, *a city,* urbanity

Vacca, *a cow,* vaccination
Valeo, *I am strong,* prevail
Veho, *I carry,* vehicle
Velox, *swift,* velocity
Venio, *I come,* advent
Venter, *the belly,* ventriloquism
Ver, *the spring,* vernal
Verbum, *a word,* verbal
Vertex, *the top,* vertical
Verto, *I turn,* convert
Verus, *true,* verity
Vestis, *a garment,* vestal
Vetus, *old,* veteran
Via, *a way,* deviate
Vibro, *I shake,* vibrate
Video, *I see,* visible
Vigil, *watchful,* vigilant
Vinco, *I conquer,* invincible
Vindex, *defender,* vindicate
Vita, *life,* vital
Vivo, *I live,* survive
Volo, *I will,* voluntary
Voco, *I call,* revoke
Volo, *I fly,* volatile
Volvo, *I roll,* revolve
Voveo, *I vow,* vote
Vox, *a voice,* vocal
Vulcanus, *the god of fire,* volcano
Vulgus, *the rabble,* vulgar

GREEK ROOTS WITH ENGLISH DERIVATIVES.

Aer, *the air,* aërial
Agogos, *a leader,* demagogue
Akouo, *I hear,* acoustics
Aner, *a man,* monandria
Anthos, *a flower,* anthology
Anthropos, *a man,* anthropology
Archo, *I rule,* anarchy
Arctos, *a bear,* arctic
Aristos, *best,* aristocracy
Arithmos, *number,* arithmetic
Astron, *a star,* astronomy
Atmos, *vapour,* atmosphere
Bapto, *I dip,* baptise
Baros, *weight,* barometer
Biblos, *a book,* Bible
Bios, *life,* biography
Botane, *a herb,* botany
Chalyps, *steel,* chalybeate
Chloros, *green,* chloride
Christos, *anointed,* Christ

Chronos, *time,* chronometer
Demos, *the people,* epidemic
Dendron, *a tree,* rhododendron
Doxa, *opinion,* orthodox
Drus, *an oak,* Druid
Dynamis, *power,* dynamics
Ecleipo, *I fail,* ecliptic
Eidos, *a form,* idol
Entoma, *insects,* entomology
Epos, *a word,* epic
Etumos, *true,* etymology
Gala, *milk,* galaxy
Gamos, *marriage,* bigamy
Ge, *the earth,* geography
Gennao, *I produce,* oxygen
Glotta, *the tongue,* glossary
Glupho, *I carve,* hieroglyphics
Gonia, *corner,* polygon
Gramma, *a letter,* grammar
Grapho, *I write,* autograph

GREEK ROOTS WITH ENGLISH DERIVATIVES—*continued.*

Gune, *a woman*, monogynia
Hedra, *a seat*, cathedral
Helios, *the sun*, aphelion
Hemera, *a day*, ephemeral
Hemisus, *half*, hemisphere
Heteros, *different*, heterodox
Hieros, *holy*, hierarchy
Hippos, *a horse*, hippopotamus
Hodos, *a way*, exodus
Holos, *the whole*, catholic
Homos, *similar*, homologous
Hudor, *water*, hydrostatics
Isos, *equal*, isosceles
Kakos, *bad*, cacophony
Kalos, *handsome*, kaleidoscope
Kalypto, *I cover*, apocalypse
Kratos, *strength*, aristocracy
Kreas, *flesh*, pancreatic
Kryptos, *hidden*, crypt
Kyklos, *a circle*, cycle
Kylindo, *I roll*, cylinder
Laos, *the people*, laity
Lithos, *a stone*, lithography
Logos, *a word*, catalogue
Lusis, *a loosening*, analyse
Martyr, *a witness*, martyr
Mathema, *science*, mathematics
Mechane, *a machine*, mechanics
Melan, *black*, melancholy
Melos, *a song*, melody
Meter, *a mother*, metropolis
Metron, *a measure*, geometry
Micros, *little*, microscope
Misos, *hatred*, misanthrope
Monos, *alone*, monosyllable
Morphe, *shape*, metamorphosis
Mythos, *a fable*, mythology
Naus, *a ship*, nautical
Nekros, *dead*, necromancy
Neos, *new*, neology
Nesos, *an island*, Polynesia
Nitron, *nitre*, nitrogen
Nomos, *a law*, astronomy
Octo, *eight*, octave
Ode, *a song*, prosody
Oikos, *a house*, economy
Oligos, *few*, oligarchy
Oon, *an egg*, oolite
Optomai, *I see*, optics
Organon, *an instrument*, organic
Ornis, *a bird*, ornithology

Orthos, *right*, orthography
Oxys, *acid*, oxygen
Pais, *a boy*, pedagogue
Pas, *all*, panoply
Pathos, *feeling*, pathetic
Petalon, *a leaf*, petal
Petros, *a stone*, petrifaction
Phaino, *I appear*, phenomenon
Phemi, *I speak*, blaspheme
Philos, *a friend*, philosophy
Phobeo, *I terrify*, hydrophobia
Phone, *a sound*, euphony
Phthongos, *a sound*, diphthong
Physis, *nature*, physical
Phyton, *a plant*, zoophyte
Polemos, *war*, polemical
Poleo, *I sell*, bibliopole
Polis, *a city*, metropolis
Polys, *many*, polygon
Poros, *a passage*, pore
Potamos, *a river*, hippopotamus
Pous, *a foot*, antipodes
Presbuteros, *elder*, presbyterian
Pteron, *a wing*, aptera
Pyr, *fire*, pyramid
Sarks, *flesh*, sarcophagus
Schizo, *I divide*, schism
Sceleros, *hard*, sclerotic
Selene, *the moon*, selenite
Sites, *corn*, parasite
Skopeo, *I see*, telescope
Sophos, *wise*, philosopher
Sphaira, *a globe*, sphere
Spora, *a seed*, spore
Stalazo, *I drop*, stalactite
Stollo, *I send*, apostle
Stereos, *solid*, stereotype
Sukon, *a fig*, sycophant
Taphos, *a tomb*, epitaph
Tasso, *I arrange*, syntax
Techne, *art*, technical
Tele, *distant*, telescope
Temno, *I cut*, atom
Tereo, *I keep*, artery
Theoreo, *I see*, theory
Theos, *God*, atheist
Thermos, *warm*, thermometer
Thesis, *a placing*, hypothesis
Topos, *a place*, topography
Zoon, *an animal*, zoology

APPENDIX A.

SYNOPSIS OF CLASSIFICATION.

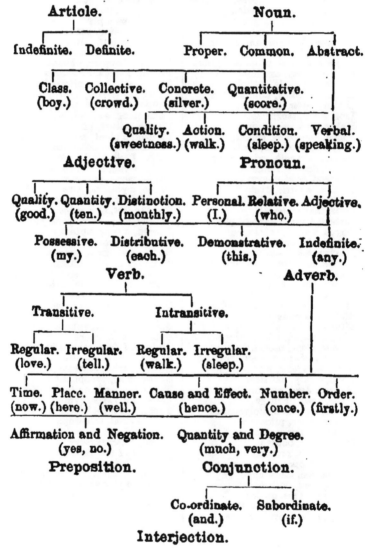

Article.

Indefinite. Definite.

Noun.

Proper. Common. Abstract.

Class. Collective. Concrete. Quantitative.
(boy.) (crowd.) (silver.) (score.)

Quality. Action. Condition. Verbal.
(sweetness.) (walk.) (sleep.) (speaking.)

Adjective.

Quality. Quantity. Distinction.
(good.) (ten.) (monthly.)

Possessive. Distributive.
(my.) (each.)

Pronoun.

Personal. Relative. Adjective.
(I.) (who.)

Demonstrative. Indefinite.
(this.) (any.)

Verb.

Transitive. Intransitive.

Regular. Irregular. Regular. Irregular.
(love.) (tell.) (walk.) (sleep.)

Adverb.

Time. Place. Manner. Cause and Effect. Number. Order.
(now.) (here.) (well.) (hence.) (once.) (firstly.)

Affirmation and Negation. Quantity and Degree.
(yes, no.) (much, very.)

Preposition.   **Conjunction.**

Co-ordinate. Subordinate.
(and.) (if.)

Interjection.

APPENDIX B.

PARSING TABLE.

	Kind					Limiting what?	Rule of Syntax
Article.	Kind.					Limiting what?	Do.
Noun.	Kind.	Gender.	Number.	Case.		Nominative to, or governed by, what?	Do.
Adjective.	Kind and degree.	Gender.	Number.	Case.		Qualifying, and agreeing with, what?	Do.
Pronoun.	Kind.	Person. Gender.	Number.	Case.		Nominative to, or governed by, what?	Do.
Verb.	Kind.	Person.	Number.	Tense.	Mood and Voice.	Agreeing with, and governing what?	Do.
Adverb.	Kind and degree.					Qualifying what?	Do.
Preposition.	Why.	Relates what?				Governs what?	Do.
Conjunction.	Kind.	Why.					Do.
Interjection.	Why.					Governs what?	Do.

APPENDIX C.

ILLUSTRATING INFLECTION.

SAXON.	LATIN.

Noun.

Tunge, a tongue, f.

	Singular.	Plural
Nom.	Tunge	tungan
Gen.	Tungan	tungena
Dat.	Tungan	tungum
Acc.	Tungan	tungan
Ab.	Tungan	tungum

Noun.

Lingua, a tongue, f.

	Singular.	Plural.
Nom.	Lingua	linguae
Gen.	Linguae	linguarum
Dat.	Linguae	linguis
Acc.	Linguam	linguas
V.	Lingua	linguae
A.	Lingua	linguis

Adjective.

God, good.

Singular.

	M.	F.	N.
N.	God	—	—
G.	God-es	re	es
D.	God-um	re	um
A.	God-ne	e	—
Ab.	God-e	e	e

Plural

N.	God-e	god-e	—
G.	God-ra	ra	ra
D.	God-um	um	um
A.	God-e	e	—
Ab.	God-um	um	um

Adjective.

Bonus, good.

Singular.

	M.	F.	N.
N.	Bon-us	a	um
G.	Bon-i	ae	i
D.	Bon-o	ae	o
A.	Bon-um	am	um
V.	Bon-e	a	um
A.	Bon-o	a	o

Plural.

N.	Bon-i	ae	a
G.	Bon-orum	arum	orum
D.	Bon-is	is	is
A.	Bon-os	as	a
V.	Bon-i	ae	a
A.	Bon-is	is	is

Verb.

Lufige, to love.

(Present Tense.)

Singular.

Io	Luf-ige	I love
Thu	Luf-ast	thou lovest
He	Luf-ath	he loves

Plural.

We	Luf-iath	we love
Ge	Luf-iath	you love
He	Luf-iath	they love

Verb.

Amare, to love.

(Present Tense.)

Singular.

Am-o	I love
Am-as	thou lovest
Am-at	he loves

Plural.

Am-amus	we love
Am-atis	you love
Am-ant	they love

THE END.

CPSIA information can be obtained
at www.ICGtesting.com
Printed in the USA
BVHW051044210721
612411BV00012B/3674